C-2   CAREER EXAMINATION SERIES

This is your
PASSBOOK for...

Account Clerk

Test Preparation Study Guide
Questions & Answers

COPYRIGHT NOTICE

This book is SOLELY intended for, is sold ONLY to, and its use is RESTRICTED to individual, bona fide applicants or candidates who qualify by virtue of having seriously filed applications for appropriate license, certificate, professional and/or promotional advancement, higher school matriculation, scholarship, or other legitimate requirements of education and/or governmental authorities.

This book is NOT intended for use, class instruction, tutoring, training, duplication, copying, reprinting, excerption, or adaptation, etc., by:

1) Other publishers
2) Proprietors and/or Instructors of "Coaching" and/or Preparatory Courses
3) Personnel and/or Training Divisions of commercial, industrial, and governmental organizations
4) Schools, colleges, or universities and/or their departments and staffs, including teachers and other personnel
5) Testing Agencies or Bureaus
6) Study groups which seek by the purchase of a single volume to copy and/or duplicate and/or adapt this material for use by the group as a whole without having purchased individual volumes for each of the members of the group
7) Et al.

Such persons would be in violation of appropriate Federal and State statutes.

PROVISION OF LICENSING AGREEMENTS – Recognized educational, commercial, industrial, and governmental institutions and organizations, and others legitimately engaged in educational pursuits, including training, testing, and measurement activities, may address request for a licensing agreement to the copyright owners, who will determine whether, and under what conditions, including fees and charges, the materials in this book may be used them. In other words, a licensing facility exists for the legitimate use of the material in this book on other than an individual basis. However, it is asseverated and affirmed here that the material in this book CANNOT be used without the receipt of the express permission of such a licensing agreement from the Publishers. Inquiries re licensing should be addressed to the company, attention rights and permissions department.

All rights reserved, including the right of reproduction in whole or in part, in any form or by any means, electronic or mechanical, including photocopying, recording, or by any information storage and retrieval system, without permission in writing from the Publisher.

Copyright © 2024 by
National Learning Corporation

212 Michael Drive, Syosset, NY 11791
(516) 921-8888 • www.passbooks.com
E-mail: info@passbooks.com

PUBLISHED IN THE UNITED STATES OF AMERICA

PASSBOOK® SERIES

THE *PASSBOOK® SERIES* has been created to prepare applicants and candidates for the ultimate academic battlefield – the examination room.

At some time in our lives, each and every one of us may be required to take an examination – for validation, matriculation, admission, qualification, registration, certification, or licensure.

Based on the assumption that every applicant or candidate has met the basic formal educational standards, has taken the required number of courses, and read the necessary texts, the *PASSBOOK® SERIES* furnishes the one special preparation which may assure passing with confidence, instead of failing with insecurity. Examination questions – together with answers – are furnished as the basic vehicle for study so that the mysteries of the examination and its compounding difficulties may be eliminated or diminished by a sure method.

This book is meant to help you pass your examination provided that you qualify and are serious in your objective.

The entire field is reviewed through the huge store of content information which is succinctly presented through a provocative and challenging approach – the question-and-answer method.

A climate of success is established by furnishing the correct answers at the end of each test.

You soon learn to recognize types of questions, forms of questions, and patterns of questioning. You may even begin to anticipate expected outcomes.

You perceive that many questions are repeated or adapted so that you can gain acute insights, which may enable you to score many sure points.

You learn how to confront new questions, or types of questions, and to attack them confidently and work out the correct answers.

You note objectives and emphases, and recognize pitfalls and dangers, so that you may make positive educational adjustments.

Moreover, you are kept fully informed in relation to new concepts, methods, practices, and directions in the field.

You discover that you are actually taking the examination all the time: you are preparing for the examination by "taking" an examination, not by reading extraneous and/or supererogatory textbooks.

In short, this PASSBOOK®, used directedly, should be an important factor in helping you to pass your test.

ACCOUNT CLERK

DUTIES:
The work involves performing specialized clerical work in keeping financial records of some variety and complexity. Using a single or double entry system, an employee in this class keeps books or records subject to audit. Duties may include utilization of computers or word processors with financial capabilities. The work is performed in accordance with clearly established accounting methods and procedures and is reviewed primarily through verification of financial records and statements. The employee in this class receives remittances by mail or in person; verifies amount, computes interest and penalties and posts to book or original entry; assists in maintaining labor, material and operational cost records; issues receipts for monies received; classifies constantly recurring receipts and expenditures and distributes costs according to prescribed code; and operates computing, calculating, check writing and other office machines. Supervision may be exercised over a small number of subordinate clerical personnel. Does related work as required.

EXAMPLES OF WORK:
Reviews a variety of documents such as claim forms, vouchers, bills, purchase orders, to determine eligibility for payment or to verify accuracy of payment made, according to defined procedures and policies; verifies all calculations and codes on documents; posts figures to appropriate accounts either manually or through a computer, verifying all data entered; reconciles all entries, both debits and credits; prepares simple financial or statistical reports from data entered, including status of accounts, current balances, cash received or paid; produces data needed for state and federal reimbursement claims; receives cash payments, issues receipts; prepares checks for disbursement, deposits funds into appropriate accounts, prepares reconciliation of balances and posts balances to appropriate ledgers; makes bank deposits as necessary; contacts clients, vendors, etc., to obtain additional information as necessary; provides routine information orally or in writing in response to inquiries on financial records; files and maintains all related records such as records related to processing of payrolls, invoices, vouchers, bills, correspondence; receives, balances, audits, and prepares payroll time records; processes data either for computer or other records; makes computations as necessary; operates calculator, computer terminal, printer and other related office equipment.

SCOPE OF THE EXAMINATION
The written test will cover knowledge, skills and/or abilities in such areas as:
1. **Clerical operations with letters and numbers** - These questions test your skills and abilities in clerical operations involving alphabetizing, comparing, checking and counting. The questions require you to follow the specific directions given for each question which may involve alphabetizing, comparing, checking and counting given groups of letters and/or numbers.
2. **Arithmetic computation** - These questions test your ability to do addition, subtraction, multiplication, and division. Questions may also involve fractions, decimals, averages, and percents.
3. **Arithmetic reasoning** - These questions test your ability to solve an arithmetic problem presented in sentence or short paragraph form. You must read the problem, understand the situation presented, decide what must be done to solve it, and apply the appropriate arithmetic operation(s) in the appropriate order in order to determine the correct solution. Knowledge of addition, subtraction, multiplication, and division is necessary. Questions may also involve the use of percents, decimals, and fractions.

HOW TO PREPARE GUIDE FOR
ACCOUNT CLERK
WRITTEN EXAMINATION

I. **INTRODUCTION**

The purpose of these instructions is to help you prepare for the written, entry-level qualifying examination which is being given for the Account Clerk classification. The Account Clerk Qualifying Exam is the exam you are taking in order to be hired as an Account Clerk.

It is very important that you sit down in a quiet place and review the material in this booklet. You should also set aside time to practice doing the things that are suggested in this booklet to prepare for the Qualifying Exam. Please remember that the material in this booklet is designed to help you prepare for the exam. You will not need the material in this booklet at the time you actually take the exam. Therefore, you will not be allowed to carry this booklet into the exam session. Later in this booklet, we will instruct you on what you are allowed to bring to the exam session and what you **must** bring to the exam session. You will not be allowed to bring this booklet to the exam with you.

II. **JOB PREVIEW**

Account Clerks are responsible for the performance of moderately difficult clerical accounting functions. Work at this level contrasts with the routine record keeping tasks assigned other clerical positions by the addition of difficult and responsible accounting-related clerical duties. As incumbents gain experience, more complex accounting duties are assigned. Work requires use of some judgment and interpretation of departmental and fiscal policies and regulations and consideration of alternatives. Employees make decisions based on applicable functions, rules, and regulations of the organization and solve problems identified by others. Work is reviewed to determine compliance with established rules, regulations, and procedures and may also involve technical guidance and minor supervision over clerical employees.

III. **PREPARING FOR THE EXAM**

    A. General Information on What to do Before the Exam

    Here are some suggestions for what to do before the exam and for getting to the testing location on time and with the proper things that you will need to take the test.

- Be well rested. Get a good night's sleep for several nights in a row before the written exam.

- Allow plenty of time to get to the exam site. If you are rushed and late, you may be upset when you get there. Plan to arrive at least 20 minutes before the exam start time.

- Do not bring a cell phone to the testing site. Pagers should only be brought if it is absolutely necessary. All pagers must be set to the vibration mode.

- Come dress comfortably. The total time provided for completion of the exam will be three hours.

- You should read and study this booklet. You should practice the kind of things that this booklet suggests that you practice.

- Do **not** bring this or any other booklets, reading, or study materials to the exam. You **will not** be permitted to bring them in. All materials needed to complete the exam will be given to you at the exam.

- You **must** bring the Exam Notification Letter or Notification Postcard that you received from the Personnel Department to the examination site.

- To protect your own interests, you will also be asked to bring Picture Identification to the examination site. This may be a valid driver's license, a military identification card, a student identification card, or some other form of Picture Identification. You only need one form of Picture Identification.

- You **will not be allowed** to enter the examination site or take the exam without your Notification Letter/Postcard **and** Picture Identification.

- Bring several number 2 pencils with erasers to the exam. It is also recommended that you bring a highlighter pen and a calculator. You may bring a calculator to use for the examination. Small solar powered or battery operated calculators that perform basic functions such as addition, subtraction, multiplication, division, square roots, or percentages are allowed. Calculators that plug in, utilize tape, have word processing, spelling, thesauruses, or other storage and retrieval capabilities (except basic memory functions) are not allowed. **Calculators that are a feature on a cell phone are not permitted.** Calculators are subject to inspection by exam monitors. Applicants may not borrow or share calculators at the exam site.

B. General Information on What to do During the Examination

Some people are nervous when they take tests. There is nothing wrong with that. Whenever you are going to do something important, it is good to feel a bit keyed-up. It is nature's way of getting you warmed up and ready, like an actress or actor about to go on stage for a performance. However, it is not good to be so nervous that all you can think about is how nervous you are. You need to keep your mind on the test questions, and not on your feelings. To improve your ability to do that, you will find ideas in this booklet on how to study and prepare for the written exam. **The more**

prepared you are, the more comfortable and less nervous you will feel during the exam.

- In an exam like this one, some questions are easy and some are hard. Don't give up. Probably no one will make a perfect score. If it is hard for you to figure out an answer, it is probably hard for other people too. Keep your mind on the test, and try to answer every question. Mark an answer on your answer sheet even if it is a guess. **You will not be penalized for guessing.** On the other hand, do not spend too much time on any one question just because it is hard. This may not leave you enough time to answer questions that you know.

- You will have three hours to complete the exam. Use your time efficiently. The exam is not a test of how quickly you can answer the questions. However, it does not allow you all the time you might like to have. In the parts of the test that require reading, try to keep a steady pace. Try to finish as much of the test as you can.

- An examination monitor will be at your test site when you report. The monitor will check your Picture Identification and Exam Notification Letter/Postcard, and then will provide you with test materials. You **must** follow the instructions of the monitor at all times.

- The examination monitor will provide you with instructions concerning restroom availability during the test administration. It is important to remember that the time that you take to use the restroom is time away from working on the examination. So, we recommend that you use the restroom before the examination, if possible.

- You are not to open the examination booklets or instructions or begin working on the exam until you are instructed by the monitor to do so.

- The only materials you need to bring to the test site are a Picture Identification, Exam Notification Letter/Postcard, several number 2 pencils. You may bring a calculator to use for the Account Clerk examination. Small solar powered or battery operated calculators that perform basic functions such as addition, subtraction, multiplication, division, square roots, or percentages are allowed. Calculators that plug in, utilize tape, have word processing, spelling, thesauruses, or other storage and retrieval capabilities (except basic memory functions) are not allowed. **Calculators that are a feature on a cell phone are not permitted.** Calculators are subject to inspection by exam monitors. Applicants may not borrow or share calculators at the exam site. No other materials will be allowed in the test site.

- Candidates making any disturbances or caught cheating will be disqualified from the exam.

- Test monitors can answer questions concerning exam administration issues only. They **will not** be able to interpret exam questions for you.

- You should always check to make sure that your answers to questions are marked in the location on the answer sheet that matches the number of the question you are answering.

- If you have time remaining after you have completed the test, it is always a good idea to review your responses on the more difficult questions. Once you have finished, notify the monitor for instructions.

In summary, there are two things you can do that make you feel more comfortable taking the exam: (1) follow the guidelines presented in this booklet on how to prepare for the exam, and (2) become familiar with the kinds of questions that will be used in the exam.

IV. EXAM INFORMATION

A. General Exam Information

A study of the Account Clerk classification was conducted prior to developing the examination. A number of employees who work in this position and their supervisors participated in this study. The study showed that the following knowledges and abilities are associated with the above duties. These knowledges and abilities are needed on the first day of work before training.

- **Knowledge of bookkeeping such as reconciliations, journal entries, journal vouchers, debits, credits, accounts payable, and accounts receivable as needed to check invoices for accuracy, process vouchers, record financial transactions, and make corrections to financial records.**

- **Knowledge of accounting terminology such as debits, credits, general ledgers, warrants, and journal vouchers as needed to communicate with accounting personnel/vendors and document financial transactions.**

- **Knowledge of filing systems such as alphanumeric, alphabetical, chronological, etc. as needed to ensure easy retrieval and meet record retention requirements.**

- Ability to operate a computer as needed to access/retrieve/store information, prepare letters, memos, etc., enter data, generate reports, prepare spreadsheets, process payment transactions, and provide/receive information through email.

- **Ability to read and comprehend narrative information such as correspondence, departmental manuals, contracts, bids, bid specifications, state and federal regulations, and catalogs as needed to ensure compliance with rules and regulations, provide requested information, and remain current on departmental procedures and requirements.**

- **Ability to perform basic math to include adding, subtraction, multiplication, division, percentages as needed to verify invoices,**

calculate costs, calculate leave balances, conduct inventory, determine refunds, order supplies, provide budget estimates, balance purchase orders, and prepare requisitions.

- Ability to operate office equipment such as copier, fax, printer, scanner, telephone, calculator, cash register and shredder as needed to maximize work time, receive and transmit information, and store and analyze information.

- Ability to follow oral and written instructions as needed to accomplish assigned tasks and responsibilities and comply with appropriate policies and procedures.

- Ability to communicate orally to vendors, general public, co-workers, other state agencies, and supervisor as needed to answer questions, provide/obtain information/instructions, request assistance, and resolve discrepancies.

- **Ability to pay close attention to detail as needed to verify invoices and ensure proper completion of documents.**

- Ability to establish and maintain effective working relationships with vendors, co-workers, other state agencies, general public, and supervisor as needed to achieve departmental/agency goals, promote teamwork, and maximize goods and services.

- Ability to be flexible as needed to accomplish assigned work and perform additional duties in absence of co-workers or as needed.

- Ability to work on multiple tasks simultaneously as needed to meet deadlines and ensure required tasks are accomplished.

- Ability to plan and organize to include time management and prioritizing tasks as needed to meet deadlines and achieve objectives.

- Ability to maintain confidentiality as needed to ensure employee/client privacy and comply with department/state/federal requirements.

- **Ability to compose correspondence such as letters, memos, and reports to include utilizing proper sentence structured, grammar, punctuation, and spelling as needed to provide/request information, respond to inquiries, obtain equipment and supplies, and maintain documentation for auditing purposes.**

- **Ability to file documents such as employee records, purchase orders, requisitions, vouchers, and inventory records as needed to retrieve in a timely manner, maintain documentation, and ensure accessibility for future reference.**

- **Ability to compare information such as invoices to shipping tickets, requisitions to purchase orders, and leave slips to leave reports as** needed to identify/correct errors, and ensure balance.

- Ability to maintain accurate records as needed to ensure appropriate documentation and meet documentation requirements.

- **Ability to proof documents as needed to verify accuracy and identify errors.**

- Ability to work independently with minimal supervision as needed to perform assigned tasks and meet required deadlines.

The examination for Account Clerk will measure the knowledges and abilities above that appear in **bold print**. The remaining knowledges and abilities must be demonstrated during the probationary period if you are hired into an Account Clerk position.

V. ADDITIONAL INFORMATION FOR TAKING THIS EXAM

A. Effective Note Taking

Why Take Notes?

There are several good reasons to take notes:

- Taking notes can help you remember; notes you take in your own words are easier to understand and remember.

- Writing down notes may actually make ideas you did not fully understand clearer.

Taking Effective Notes

The following are some rules and suggestions for taking effective notes:

- Make your notes brief. Pick out the important points.

- Do not use a sentence when you can use a phrase. Do not use a phrase when you can use a word.

- Use abbreviations whenever possible.

- Put most notes in your own words. However, copy the following exactly as they are presented:

    a. Definitionsd
    b. Specific Facts
    c. Specific Rules and Procedures

B. Strategies For Taking the Exam

By following the suggestions listed below, you can do your best:

- Read the questions carefully. Be sure you know what the question asks and what the choices say before you try to answer the question. On every test, people choose wrong answers simply because they failed to pay attention to part of the question or failed to read all of the answer.

- Choose the answer that is generally best. To keep questions short, they cannot have a lot of detail. You should give the answer that would be considered to be generally the best.

- For "Reading Comprehension" questions, decide something about each question.

    1. You may decide you know the answer. Mark your answer on the answer sheet. Spend no more time on that question.

    2. You may decide you are fairly sure of the answer, but may want to think more about it. Mark your answer sheet and make a note of it in the test booklet so it will be easier to find later.

    3. You may decide one or two answers are definitely not the best. Eliminate the answers you know are wrong then direct your attention to those choices that are potentially correct.

    4. You may decide that figuring out the answer is possible, but will take you a lot of time. Don't mark any answer. Note the question in your test booklet so you can find it when you are ready to come back to it. Make sure you finish the test in enough time to come back to answer the question.

    5. You may decide you don't know the answer and that all you can do is make a guess. Make the guess. Mark the answer sheet to show your answer. Don't waste any more time on that question. There is no penalty for guessing and sometimes you may guess right.

- Don't change answers unless you have a good reason. When people change their answers, they more often change from a right answer to a wrong one rather than from a wrong answer to a right one. The reason seems to be that they start thinking about some specific case, which results in choosing an answer on the basis of facts that are not given in the question. Or, people think about what some part of a question says and forget about what the rest of the question said.

- Use your time efficiently. You may not have all of the time you might like to complete the test. In the parts of the test that require reading, read at a normal pace so that you can finish the test and have time to go back and work on the questions you saved until last.

- Don't give up. Many people give up too easily on test questions. If the question looks too hard, they don't even try. Look for the specific information needed to answer the question. However, do not spend too much time on any one question just because it is hard. Doing that may not leave you enough time to give the answers that you know.

C. Study Suggestions

You may find some of the following ideas helpful in preparing for the exam:

- Do not prepare for the exam in a single session.

- Study in a quiet place. Do not study when you are doing something else.

- Make up your own tests and take them.

- Pretend that you are in a real testing situation and try not to talk to anyone else while you are taking the sample tests.

- Practice following instructions. Read sections of how-to books or instruction manuals you may have at home and practice taking notes or highlighting important aspects of the sections.

- Study the sample test items in this booklet.

- Study whatever material you believe will assist you in learning each of the duties, and knowledges, skills, and abilities required for the Account Clerk position.

VI. EXAM ADMINISTRATION INFORMATION

A. What to Bring to the Examination

- Do **not** bring this booklet to the exam location. You will not be permitted to bring it in the testing room.

- Do **not** bring any of your study materials to the exam. This includes notes, manuals, and other study materials.

- Remember to bring to the exam the Notification Letter/Postcard that you received from the Personnel Department. You will **not be allowed** to take the exam without your Notification Letter/Postcard.

- To protect your own interests, you will also be asked to bring a Picture Identification to the exam location. This might be a valid driver's license, a military identification card, a student identification card, or some form of picture identification. You only need one form of Picture Identification.

- Bring several number 2 pencils with erasers to the exam. It is also recommended that you bring a highliter pen and a calculator.

- Remember, you will **not be allowed** to enter the exam location or take the exam without your Notification Letter/Postcard **and** Picture Identification.

B. Taking the Exam

You will be given three hours to complete the exam. Use your time efficiently. The exam is not a test of how quickly you can answer questions. However, it does not allow you the time you might like to have. In the parts of the test that require reading, try to keep a steady pace. Try to finish as much of the test as you can.

While reading passages, you may want to take a few notes. Make your notes brief. You may also want to underline or highlight important information as you read.

Don't give up. Many people give up too easily on tests. If the question or problem seems hard, they do not even try. Mark an answer on your answer sheet even if it is a guess. You will not be penalized for guessing. On the other hand, do not spend too much time on any one question just because it is hard. This may not leave you enough time to answer questions that you know.

VII. EXAMINATION DESCRIPTION

The Qualifying Examination will last three hours. When you read the word "exam" in the rest of these Instructions and Notes, it is a short way of referring to the entire Qualifying Examination.

You will find examples of exam items below. Please review these items in order to familiarize yourself with the kinds of items you will be asked and the format of the exam.

VIII. SAMPLE TEST ITEMS

The examination for Account Clerk will measure the knowledges and abilities above that appear in **bold print**. The following are examples of how your knowledge and abilities will be measured.

1. The general ledger of Company A is $360.00. The bank's statement, issued on the same day, shows bank charges of $8.00. Uncleared checks amount to $175.00 and the last deposit entered in the general ledger has not been credited by the bank. The amount of the deposit is $50.00. What is the balance on the bank statement?
   A. $277.00   B. $427.00   C. $469.00   D. $477.00

1.____

2. Tribble, William T. would be filed between
   A. Tribble, Joseph and Tribble, Thomas
   B. Tribble, Peter and Tribble, Zachary
   C. Tribble, Walter and Tribble, Wilhelm
   D. Tribbel, W. and Tribbel, James

   2.____

3. A chronological record of all transactions of a business is a(n)
   A. journal   B. chart   C. invoice   D. receipt

   3.____

4. State law requires the Division of Purchasing to request sealed bids for purchases involving more than the minimum amount prescribed by law except in emergency situations or as otherwise provided by law. All bids shall be sealed when received and shall be opened in public. A bid not properly identified at bid opening will be disqualified. Bids properly identified in accordance with the terms and conditions of the Invitation to Bid (ITB) will be securely kept, unopened until the stated opening date and hour. The Division of Purchasing accepts no responsibility for premature opening of a bid not properly identified or late arrival of a bid for whatever reason. At the hour stated in the notice, all bids shall be opened in public for information of interested parties who may be present either in person or by representative. Such information is not to be construed as meaning any bid meets all specifications set out in the ITB.
   According to the preceding passage, when is the Division of Purchasing required to request sealed bids?
   A. Purchases over $1,000
   B. Purchases over the minimum amount set by law
   C. Emergency situations
   D. At the beginning of the fiscal year

   4.____

Questions 5.

DIRECTIONS: In this section, there are questions that involve the comparison of various types of information. Compare the "copy" on the right against the "original" on the left and determine the number of errors, if any, in each set of data. Assume that the "original" is always correct.

ORIGINAL	COPY
Schedule for Quarterly Requisitions	Schedule of Quarterly Requisitions
January 5	January 5
April 25	April 15
July 20	July 20
October 15	October 15

5. How many errors are found in the COPY above?
   A. 0   B. 1
   C. 2   D. None of the above

   5.____

6. Select the sentence that BEST represents Standard English usage. 6.____
    A. The clerk should have known that he hadn't out to ask for supplies without a requisition.
    B. The clerk should have known that he ought not to have asked for supplies without a requisition.
    C. The clerk should have known that he should not of asked for supplies without a requisition.
    D. The clerk should of known that he ought not to ask for supplies without a requisition.

KEY (CORRECT ANSWERS)

1. D
2. B
3. A
4. B
5. C
6. B

HOW TO TAKE A TEST

I. YOU MUST PASS AN EXAMINATION

A. *WHAT EVERY CANDIDATE SHOULD KNOW*

Examination applicants often ask us for help in preparing for the written test. What can I study in advance? What kinds of questions will be asked? How will the test be given? How will the papers be graded?

As an applicant for a civil service examination, you may be wondering about some of these things. Our purpose here is to suggest effective methods of advance study and to describe civil service examinations.

Your chances for success on this examination can be increased if you know how to prepare. Those "pre-examination jitters" can be reduced if you know what to expect. You can even experience an adventure in good citizenship if you know why civil service exams are given.

B. *WHY ARE CIVIL SERVICE EXAMINATIONS GIVEN?*

Civil service examinations are important to you in two ways. As a citizen, you want public jobs filled by employees who know how to do their work. As a job seeker, you want a fair chance to compete for that job on an equal footing with other candidates. The best-known means of accomplishing this two-fold goal is the competitive examination.

Exams are widely publicized throughout the nation. They may be administered for jobs in federal, state, city, municipal, town or village governments or agencies.

Any citizen may apply, with some limitations, such as the age or residence of applicants. Your experience and education may be reviewed to see whether you meet the requirements for the particular examination. When these requirements exist, they are reasonable and applied consistently to all applicants. Thus, a competitive examination may cause you some uneasiness now, but it is your privilege and safeguard.

C. *HOW ARE CIVIL SERVICE EXAMS DEVELOPED?*

Examinations are carefully written by trained technicians who are specialists in the field known as "psychological measurement," in consultation with recognized authorities in the field of work that the test will cover. These experts recommend the subject matter areas or skills to be tested; only those knowledges or skills important to your success on the job are included. The most reliable books and source materials available are used as references. Together, the experts and technicians judge the difficulty level of the questions.

Test technicians know how to phrase questions so that the problem is clearly stated. Their ethics do not permit "trick" or "catch" questions. Questions may have been tried out on sample groups, or subjected to statistical analysis, to determine their usefulness.

Written tests are often used in combination with performance tests, ratings of training and experience, and oral interviews. All of these measures combine to form the best-known means of finding the right person for the right job.

II. HOW TO PASS THE WRITTEN TEST

A. NATURE OF THE EXAMINATION

To prepare intelligently for civil service examinations, you should know how they differ from school examinations you have taken. In school you were assigned certain definite pages to read or subjects to cover. The examination questions were quite detailed and usually emphasized memory. Civil service exams, on the other hand, try to discover your present ability to perform the duties of a position, plus your potentiality to learn these duties. In other words, a civil service exam attempts to predict how successful you will be. Questions cover such a broad area that they cannot be as minute and detailed as school exam questions.

In the public service similar kinds of work, or positions, are grouped together in one "class." This process is known as *position-classification*. All the positions in a class are paid according to the salary range for that class. One class title covers all of these positions, and they are all tested by the same examination.

B. FOUR BASIC STEPS

1) Study the announcement

How, then, can you know what subjects to study? Our best answer is: "Learn as much as possible about the class of positions for which you've applied." The exam will test the knowledge, skills and abilities needed to do the work.

Your most valuable source of information about the position you want is the official exam announcement. This announcement lists the training and experience qualifications. Check these standards and apply only if you come reasonably close to meeting them.

The brief description of the position in the examination announcement offers some clues to the subjects which will be tested. Think about the job itself. Review the duties in your mind. Can you perform them, or are there some in which you are rusty? Fill in the blank spots in your preparation.

Many jurisdictions preview the written test in the exam announcement by including a section called "Knowledge and Abilities Required," "Scope of the Examination," or some similar heading. Here you will find out specifically what fields will be tested.

2) Review your own background

Once you learn in general what the position is all about, and what you need to know to do the work, ask yourself which subjects you already know fairly well and which need improvement. You may wonder whether to concentrate on improving your strong areas or on building some background in your fields of weakness. When the announcement has specified "some knowledge" or "considerable knowledge," or has used adjectives like "beginning principles of…" or "advanced … methods," you can get a clue as to the number and difficulty of questions to be asked in any given field. More questions, and hence broader coverage, would be included for those subjects which are more important in the work. Now weigh your strengths and weaknesses against the job requirements and prepare accordingly.

3) Determine the level of the position

Another way to tell how intensively you should prepare is to understand the level of the job for which you are applying. Is it the entering level? In other words, is this the position in which beginners in a field of work are hired? Or is it an intermediate or advanced level? Sometimes this is indicated by such words as "Junior" or "Senior" in the class title. Other jurisdictions use Roman numerals to designate the level – Clerk I, Clerk II, for example. The word "Supervisor" sometimes appears in the title. If the level is not indicated by the title, check the description of duties. Will you be working under very close supervision, or will you have responsibility for independent decisions in this work?

4) Choose appropriate study materials

Now that you know the subjects to be examined and the relative amount of each subject to be covered, you can choose suitable study materials. For beginning level jobs, or even advanced ones, if you have a pronounced weakness in some aspect of your training, read a modern, standard textbook in that field. Be sure it is up to date and has general coverage. Such books are normally available at your library, and the librarian will be glad to help you locate one. For entry-level positions, questions of appropriate difficulty are chosen – neither highly advanced questions, nor those too simple. Such questions require careful thought but not advanced training.

If the position for which you are applying is technical or advanced, you will read more advanced, specialized material. If you are already familiar with the basic principles of your field, elementary textbooks would waste your time. Concentrate on advanced textbooks and technical periodicals. Think through the concepts and review difficult problems in your field.

These are all general sources. You can get more ideas on your own initiative, following these leads. For example, training manuals and publications of the government agency which employs workers in your field can be useful, particularly for technical and professional positions. A letter or visit to the government department involved may result in more specific study suggestions, and certainly will provide you with a more definite idea of the exact nature of the position you are seeking.

III. KINDS OF TESTS

Tests are used for purposes other than measuring knowledge and ability to perform specified duties. For some positions, it is equally important to test ability to make adjustments to new situations or to profit from training. In others, basic mental abilities not dependent on information are essential. Questions which test these things may not appear as pertinent to the duties of the position as those which test for knowledge and information. Yet they are often highly important parts of a fair examination. For very general questions, it is almost impossible to help you direct your study efforts. What we can do is to point out some of the more common of these general abilities needed in public service positions and describe some typical questions.

1) General information

Broad, general information has been found useful for predicting job success in some kinds of work. This is tested in a variety of ways, from vocabulary lists to questions about current events. Basic background in some field of work, such as sociology or economics, may be sampled in a group of questions. Often these are principles which have become familiar to most persons through exposure rather than through formal training. It is difficult to advise you how to study for these questions; being alert to the world around you is our best suggestion.

2) Verbal ability

An example of an ability needed in many positions is verbal or language ability. Verbal ability is, in brief, the ability to use and understand words. Vocabulary and grammar tests are typical measures of this ability. Reading comprehension or paragraph interpretation questions are common in many kinds of civil service tests. You are given a paragraph of written material and asked to find its central meaning.

3) Numerical ability

Number skills can be tested by the familiar arithmetic problem, by checking paired lists of numbers to see which are alike and which are different, or by interpreting charts and graphs. In the latter test, a graph may be printed in the test booklet which you are asked to use as the basis for answering questions.

4) Observation

A popular test for law-enforcement positions is the observation test. A picture is shown to you for several minutes, then taken away. Questions about the picture test your ability to observe both details and larger elements.

5) Following directions

In many positions in the public service, the employee must be able to carry out written instructions dependably and accurately. You may be given a chart with several columns, each column listing a variety of information. The questions require you to carry out directions involving the information given in the chart.

6) Skills and aptitudes

Performance tests effectively measure some manual skills and aptitudes. When the skill is one in which you are trained, such as typing or shorthand, you can practice. These tests are often very much like those given in business school or high school courses. For many of the other skills and aptitudes, however, no short-time preparation can be made. Skills and abilities natural to you or that you have developed throughout your lifetime are being tested.

Many of the general questions just described provide all the data needed to answer the questions and ask you to use your reasoning ability to find the answers. Your best preparation for these tests, as well as for tests of facts and ideas, is to be at your physical and mental best. You, no doubt, have your own methods of getting into an exam-taking mood and keeping "in shape." The next section lists some ideas on this subject.

IV. KINDS OF QUESTIONS

Only rarely is the "essay" question, which you answer in narrative form, used in civil service tests. Civil service tests are usually of the short-answer type. Full instructions for answering these questions will be given to you at the examination. But in case this is your first experience with short-answer questions and separate answer sheets, here is what you need to know:

1) **Multiple-choice Questions**

Most popular of the short-answer questions is the "multiple choice" or "best answer" question. It can be used, for example, to test for factual knowledge, ability to solve problems or judgment in meeting situations found at work.

A multiple-choice question is normally one of three types—
- It can begin with an incomplete statement followed by several possible endings. You are to find the one ending which *best* completes the statement, although some of the others may not be entirely wrong.
- It can also be a complete statement in the form of a question which is answered by choosing one of the statements listed.

- It can be in the form of a problem – again you select the best answer.

Here is an example of a multiple-choice question with a discussion which should give you some clues as to the method for choosing the right answer:

When an employee has a complaint about his assignment, the action which will *best* help him overcome his difficulty is to
   A. discuss his difficulty with his coworkers
   B. take the problem to the head of the organization
   C. take the problem to the person who gave him the assignment
   D. say nothing to anyone about his complaint

In answering this question, you should study each of the choices to find which is best. Consider choice "A" – Certainly an employee may discuss his complaint with fellow employees, but no change or improvement can result, and the complaint remains unresolved. Choice "B" is a poor choice since the head of the organization probably does not know what assignment you have been given, and taking your problem to him is known as "going over the head" of the supervisor. The supervisor, or person who made the assignment, is the person who can clarify it or correct any injustice. Choice "C" is, therefore, correct. To say nothing, as in choice "D," is unwise. Supervisors have and interest in knowing the problems employees are facing, and the employee is seeking a solution to his problem.

2) True/False Questions

The "true/false" or "right/wrong" form of question is sometimes used. Here a complete statement is given. Your job is to decide whether the statement is right or wrong.

SAMPLE: A roaming cell-phone call to a nearby city costs less than a non-roaming call to a distant city.

This statement is wrong, or false, since roaming calls are more expensive.

This is not a complete list of all possible question forms, although most of the others are variations of these common types. You will always get complete directions for answering questions. Be sure you understand *how* to mark your answers – ask questions until you do.

V. RECORDING YOUR ANSWERS

Computer terminals are used more and more today for many different kinds of exams.
For an examination with very few applicants, you may be told to record your answers in the test booklet itself. Separate answer sheets are much more common. If this separate answer sheet is to be scored by machine – and this is often the case – it is highly important that you mark your answers correctly in order to get credit.

An electronic scoring machine is often used in civil service offices because of the speed with which papers can be scored. Machine-scored answer sheets must be marked with a pencil, which will be given to you. This pencil has a high graphite content which responds to the electronic scoring machine. As a matter of fact, stray dots may register as answers, so do not let your pencil rest on the answer sheet while you are pondering the correct answer. Also, if your pencil lead breaks or is otherwise defective, ask for another.

Since the answer sheet will be dropped in a slot in the scoring machine, be careful not to bend the corners or get the paper crumpled.

The answer sheet normally has five vertical columns of numbers, with 30 numbers to a column. These numbers correspond to the question numbers in your test booklet. After each number, going across the page are four or five pairs of dotted lines. These short dotted lines have small letters or numbers above them. The first two pairs may also have a "T" or "F" above the letters. This indicates that the first two pairs only are to be used if the questions are of the true-false type. If the questions are multiple choice, disregard the "T" and "F" and pay attention only to the small letters or numbers.

Answer your questions in the manner of the sample that follows:

32. The largest city in the United States is
    A. Washington, D.C.
    B. New York City
    C. Chicago
    D. Detroit
    E. San Francisco

1) Choose the answer you think is best. (New York City is the largest, so "B" is correct.)
2) Find the row of dotted lines numbered the same as the question you are answering. (Find row number 32)
3) Find the pair of dotted lines corresponding to the answer. (Find the pair of lines under the mark "B.")
4) Make a solid black mark between the dotted lines.

VI. BEFORE THE TEST

Common sense will help you find procedures to follow to get ready for an examination. Too many of us, however, overlook these sensible measures. Indeed, nervousness and fatigue have been found to be the most serious reasons why applicants fail to do their best on civil service tests. Here is a list of reminders:

- Begin your preparation early – Don't wait until the last minute to go scurrying around for books and materials or to find out what the position is all about.
- Prepare continuously – An hour a night for a week is better than an all-night cram session. This has been definitely established. What is more, a night a week for a month will return better dividends than crowding your study into a shorter period of time.
- Locate the place of the exam – You have been sent a notice telling you when and where to report for the examination. If the location is in a different town or otherwise unfamiliar to you, it would be well to inquire the best route and learn something about the building.
- Relax the night before the test – Allow your mind to rest. Do not study at all that night. Plan some mild recreation or diversion; then go to bed early and get a good night's sleep.
- Get up early enough to make a leisurely trip to the place for the test – This way unforeseen events, traffic snarls, unfamiliar buildings, etc. will not upset you.
- Dress comfortably – A written test is not a fashion show. You will be known by number and not by name, so wear something comfortable.

- Leave excess paraphernalia at home – Shopping bags and odd bundles will get in your way. You need bring only the items mentioned in the official notice you received; usually everything you need is provided. Do not bring reference books to the exam. They will only confuse those last minutes and be taken away from you when in the test room.
- Arrive somewhat ahead of time – If because of transportation schedules you must get there very early, bring a newspaper or magazine to take your mind off yourself while waiting.
- Locate the examination room – When you have found the proper room, you will be directed to the seat or part of the room where you will sit. Sometimes you are given a sheet of instructions to read while you are waiting. Do not fill out any forms until you are told to do so; just read them and be prepared.
- Relax and prepare to listen to the instructions
- If you have any physical problem that may keep you from doing your best, be sure to tell the test administrator. If you are sick or in poor health, you really cannot do your best on the exam. You can come back and take the test some other time.

VII. AT THE TEST

The day of the test is here and you have the test booklet in your hand. The temptation to get going is very strong. Caution! There is more to success than knowing the right answers. You must know how to identify your papers and understand variations in the type of short-answer question used in this particular examination. Follow these suggestions for maximum results from your efforts:

1) Cooperate with the monitor

The test administrator has a duty to create a situation in which you can be as much at ease as possible. He will give instructions, tell you when to begin, check to see that you are marking your answer sheet correctly, and so on. He is not there to guard you, although he will see that your competitors do not take unfair advantage. He wants to help you do your best.

2) Listen to all instructions

Don't jump the gun! Wait until you understand all directions. In most civil service tests you get more time than you need to answer the questions. So don't be in a hurry. Read each word of instructions until you clearly understand the meaning. Study the examples, listen to all announcements and follow directions. Ask questions if you do not understand what to do.

3) Identify your papers

Civil service exams are usually identified by number only. You will be assigned a number; you must not put your name on your test papers. Be sure to copy your number correctly. Since more than one exam may be given, copy your exact examination title.

4) Plan your time

Unless you are told that a test is a "speed" or "rate of work" test, speed itself is usually not important. Time enough to answer all the questions will be provided, but this does not mean that you have all day. An overall time limit has been set. Divide the total time (in minutes) by the number of questions to determine the approximate time you have for each question.

5) Do not linger over difficult questions

If you come across a difficult question, mark it with a paper clip (useful to have along) and come back to it when you have been through the booklet. One caution if you do this – be sure to skip a number on your answer sheet as well. Check often to be sure that you have not lost your place and that you are marking in the row numbered the same as the question you are answering.

6) Read the questions

Be sure you know what the question asks! Many capable people are unsuccessful because they failed to *read* the questions correctly.

7) Answer all questions

Unless you have been instructed that a penalty will be deducted for incorrect answers, it is better to guess than to omit a question.

8) Speed tests

It is often better NOT to guess on speed tests. It has been found that on timed tests people are tempted to spend the last few seconds before time is called in marking answers at random – without even reading them – in the hope of picking up a few extra points. To discourage this practice, the instructions may warn you that your score will be "corrected" for guessing. That is, a penalty will be applied. The incorrect answers will be deducted from the correct ones, or some other penalty formula will be used.

9) Review your answers

If you finish before time is called, go back to the questions you guessed or omitted to give them further thought. Review other answers if you have time.

10) Return your test materials

If you are ready to leave before others have finished or time is called, take ALL your materials to the monitor and leave quietly. Never take any test material with you. The monitor can discover whose papers are not complete, and taking a test booklet may be grounds for disqualification.

VIII. EXAMINATION TECHNIQUES

1) Read the general instructions carefully. These are usually printed on the first page of the exam booklet. As a rule, these instructions refer to the timing of the examination; the fact that you should not start work until the signal and must stop work at a signal, etc. If there are any *special* instructions, such as a choice of questions to be answered, make sure that you note this instruction carefully.

2) When you are ready to start work on the examination, that is as soon as the signal has been given, read the instructions to each question booklet, underline any key words or phrases, such as *least, best, outline, describe* and the like. In this way you will tend to answer as requested rather than discover on reviewing your paper that you *listed without describing*, that you selected the *worst* choice rather than the *best* choice, etc.

3) If the examination is of the objective or multiple-choice type – that is, each question will also give a series of possible answers: A, B, C or D, and you are called upon to select the best answer and write the letter next to that answer on your answer paper – it is advisable to start answering each question in turn. There may be anywhere from 50 to 100 such questions in the three or four hours allotted and you can see how much time would be taken if you read through all the questions before beginning to answer any. Furthermore, if you come across a question or group of questions which you know would be difficult to answer, it would undoubtedly affect your handling of all the other questions.

4) If the examination is of the essay type and contains but a few questions, it is a moot point as to whether you should read all the questions before starting to answer any one. Of course, if you are given a choice – say five out of seven and the like – then it is essential to read all the questions so you can eliminate the two that are most difficult. If, however, you are asked to answer all the questions, there may be danger in trying to answer the easiest one first because you may find that you will spend too much time on it. The best technique is to answer the first question, then proceed to the second, etc.

5) Time your answers. Before the exam begins, write down the time it started, then add the time allowed for the examination and write down the time it must be completed, then divide the time available somewhat as follows:
    - If 3-1/2 hours are allowed, that would be 210 minutes. If you have 80 objective-type questions, that would be an average of 2-1/2 minutes per question. Allow yourself no more than 2 minutes per question, or a total of 160 minutes, which will permit about 50 minutes to review.
    - If for the time allotment of 210 minutes there are 7 essay questions to answer, that would average about 30 minutes a question. Give yourself only 25 minutes per question so that you have about 35 minutes to review.

6) The most important instruction is to *read each question* and make sure you know what is wanted. The second most important instruction is to *time yourself properly* so that you answer every question. The third most important instruction is to *answer every question*. Guess if you have to but include something for each question. Remember that you will receive no credit for a blank and will probably receive some credit if you write something in answer to an essay question. If you guess a letter – say "B" for a multiple-choice question – you may have guessed right. If you leave a blank as an answer to a multiple-choice question, the examiners may respect your feelings but it will not add a point to your score. Some exams may penalize you for wrong answers, so in such cases *only*, you may not want to guess unless you have some basis for your answer.

7) Suggestions
    a. Objective-type questions
        1. Examine the question booklet for proper sequence of pages and questions
        2. Read all instructions carefully
        3. Skip any question which seems too difficult; return to it after all other questions have been answered
        4. Apportion your time properly; do not spend too much time on any single question or group of questions

5. Note and underline key words – *all, most, fewest, least, best, worst, same, opposite,* etc.
6. Pay particular attention to negatives
7. Note unusual option, e.g., unduly long, short, complex, different or similar in content to the body of the question
8. Observe the use of "hedging" words – *probably, may, most likely,* etc.
9. Make sure that your answer is put next to the same number as the question
10. Do not second-guess unless you have good reason to believe the second answer is definitely more correct
11. Cross out original answer if you decide another answer is more accurate; do not erase until you are ready to hand your paper in
12. Answer all questions; guess unless instructed otherwise
13. Leave time for review

b. Essay questions
1. Read each question carefully
2. Determine exactly what is wanted. Underline key words or phrases.
3. Decide on outline or paragraph answer
4. Include many different points and elements unless asked to develop any one or two points or elements
5. Show impartiality by giving pros and cons unless directed to select one side only
6. Make and write down any assumptions you find necessary to answer the questions
7. Watch your English, grammar, punctuation and choice of words
8. Time your answers; don't crowd material

8) Answering the essay question

Most essay questions can be answered by framing the specific response around several key words or ideas. Here are a few such key words or ideas:

M's: manpower, materials, methods, money, management
P's: purpose, program, policy, plan, procedure, practice, problems, pitfalls, personnel, public relations

a. Six basic steps in handling problems:
1. Preliminary plan and background development
2. Collect information, data and facts
3. Analyze and interpret information, data and facts
4. Analyze and develop solutions as well as make recommendations
5. Prepare report and sell recommendations
6. Install recommendations and follow up effectiveness

b. Pitfalls to avoid
1. *Taking things for granted* – A statement of the situation does not necessarily imply that each of the elements is necessarily true; for example, a complaint may be invalid and biased so that all that can be taken for granted is that a complaint has been registered

2. *Considering only one side of a situation* – Wherever possible, indicate several alternatives and then point out the reasons you selected the best one
3. *Failing to indicate follow up* – Whenever your answer indicates action on your part, make certain that you will take proper follow-up action to see how successful your recommendations, procedures or actions turn out to be
4. *Taking too long in answering any single question* – Remember to time your answers properly

IX. AFTER THE TEST

Scoring procedures differ in detail among civil service jurisdictions although the general principles are the same. Whether the papers are hand-scored or graded by machine we have described, they are nearly always graded by number. That is, the person who marks the paper knows only the number – never the name – of the applicant. Not until all the papers have been graded will they be matched with names. If other tests, such as training and experience or oral interview ratings have been given, scores will be combined. Different parts of the examination usually have different weights. For example, the written test might count 60 percent of the final grade, and a rating of training and experience 40 percent. In many jurisdictions, veterans will have a certain number of points added to their grades.

After the final grade has been determined, the names are placed in grade order and an eligible list is established. There are various methods for resolving ties between those who get the same final grade – probably the most common is to place first the name of the person whose application was received first. Job offers are made from the eligible list in the order the names appear on it. You will be notified of your grade and your rank as soon as all these computations have been made. This will be done as rapidly as possible.

People who are found to meet the requirements in the announcement are called "eligibles." Their names are put on a list of eligible candidates. An eligible's chances of getting a job depend on how high he stands on this list and how fast agencies are filling jobs from the list.

When a job is to be filled from a list of eligibles, the agency asks for the names of people on the list of eligibles for that job. When the civil service commission receives this request, it sends to the agency the names of the three people highest on this list. Or, if the job to be filled has specialized requirements, the office sends the agency the names of the top three persons who meet these requirements from the general list.

The appointing officer makes a choice from among the three people whose names were sent to him. If the selected person accepts the appointment, the names of the others are put back on the list to be considered for future openings.

That is the rule in hiring from all kinds of eligible lists, whether they are for typist, carpenter, chemist, or something else. For every vacancy, the appointing officer has his choice of any one of the top three eligibles on the list. This explains why the person whose name is on top of the list sometimes does not get an appointment when some of the persons lower on the list do. If the appointing officer chooses the second or third eligible, the No. 1 eligible does not get a job at once, but stays on the list until he is appointed or the list is terminated.

X. HOW TO PASS THE INTERVIEW TEST

The examination for which you applied requires an oral interview test. You have already taken the written test and you are now being called for the interview test – the final part of the formal examination.

You may think that it is not possible to prepare for an interview test and that there are no procedures to follow during an interview. Our purpose is to point out some things you can do in advance that will help you and some good rules to follow and pitfalls to avoid while you are being interviewed.

What is an interview supposed to test?

The written examination is designed to test the technical knowledge and competence of the candidate; the oral is designed to evaluate intangible qualities, not readily measured otherwise, and to establish a list showing the relative fitness of each candidate – as measured against his competitors – for the position sought. Scoring is not on the basis of "right" and "wrong," but on a sliding scale of values ranging from "not passable" to "outstanding." As a matter of fact, it is possible to achieve a relatively low score without a single "incorrect" answer because of evident weakness in the qualities being measured.

Occasionally, an examination may consist entirely of an oral test – either an individual or a group oral. In such cases, information is sought concerning the technical knowledges and abilities of the candidate, since there has been no written examination for this purpose. More commonly, however, an oral test is used to supplement a written examination.

Who conducts interviews?

The composition of oral boards varies among different jurisdictions. In nearly all, a representative of the personnel department serves as chairman. One of the members of the board may be a representative of the department in which the candidate would work. In some cases, "outside experts" are used, and, frequently, a businessman or some other representative of the general public is asked to serve. Labor and management or other special groups may be represented. The aim is to secure the services of experts in the appropriate field.

However the board is composed, it is a good idea (and not at all improper or unethical) to ascertain in advance of the interview who the members are and what groups they represent. When you are introduced to them, you will have some idea of their backgrounds and interests, and at least you will not stutter and stammer over their names.

What should be done before the interview?

While knowledge about the board members is useful and takes some of the surprise element out of the interview, there is other preparation which is more substantive. It *is* possible to prepare for an oral interview – in several ways:

1) Keep a copy of your application and review it carefully before the interview

This may be the only document before the oral board, and the starting point of the interview. Know what education and experience you have listed there, and the sequence and dates of all of it. Sometimes the board will ask you to review the highlights of your experience for them; you should not have to hem and haw doing it.

2) Study the class specification and the examination announcement

Usually, the oral board has one or both of these to guide them. The qualities, characteristics or knowledges required by the position sought are stated in these documents. They offer valuable clues as to the nature of the oral interview. For example, if the job involves supervisory responsibilities, the announcement will usually indicate that knowledge of modern supervisory methods and the qualifications of the candidate as a supervisor will be tested. If so, you can expect such questions, frequently in the form of a hypothetical situation which you are expected to solve. NEVER go into an oral without knowledge of the duties and responsibilities of the job you seek.

3) Think through each qualification required

Try to visualize the kind of questions you would ask if you were a board member. How well could you answer them? Try especially to appraise your own knowledge and background in each area, *measured against the job sought*, and identify any areas in which you are weak. Be critical and realistic – do not flatter yourself.

4) Do some general reading in areas in which you feel you may be weak

For example, if the job involves supervision and your past experience has NOT, some general reading in supervisory methods and practices, particularly in the field of human relations, might be useful. Do NOT study agency procedures or detailed manuals. The oral board will be testing your understanding and capacity, not your memory.

5) Get a good night's sleep and watch your general health and mental attitude

You will want a clear head at the interview. Take care of a cold or any other minor ailment, and of course, no hangovers.

What should be done on the day of the interview?

Now comes the day of the interview itself. Give yourself plenty of time to get there. Plan to arrive somewhat ahead of the scheduled time, particularly if your appointment is in the fore part of the day. If a previous candidate fails to appear, the board might be ready for you a bit early. By early afternoon an oral board is almost invariably behind schedule if there are many candidates, and you may have to wait. Take along a book or magazine to read, or your application to review, but leave any extraneous material in the waiting room when you go in for your interview. In any event, relax and compose yourself.

The matter of dress is important. The board is forming impressions about you – from your experience, your manners, your attitude, and your appearance. Give your personal appearance careful attention. Dress your best, but not your flashiest. Choose conservative, appropriate clothing, and be sure it is immaculate. This is a business interview, and your appearance should indicate that you regard it as such. Besides, being well groomed and properly dressed will help boost your confidence.

Sooner or later, someone will call your name and escort you into the interview room. *This is it*. From here on you are on your own. It is too late for any more preparation. But remember, you asked for this opportunity to prove your fitness, and you are here because your request was granted.

What happens when you go in?

The usual sequence of events will be as follows: The clerk (who is often the board stenographer) will introduce you to the chairman of the oral board, who will introduce you to the other members of the board. Acknowledge the introductions before you sit down. Do not be surprised if you find a microphone facing you or a stenotypist sitting by. Oral interviews are usually recorded in the event of an appeal or other review.

Usually the chairman of the board will open the interview by reviewing the highlights of your education and work experience from your application – primarily for the benefit of the other members of the board, as well as to get the material into the record. Do not interrupt or comment unless there is an error or significant misinterpretation; if that is the case, do not hesitate. But do not quibble about insignificant matters. Also, he will usually ask you some question about your education, experience or your present job – partly to get you to start talking and to establish the interviewing "rapport." He may start the actual questioning, or turn it over to one of the other members. Frequently, each member undertakes the questioning on a particular area, one in which he is perhaps most competent, so you can expect each member to participate in the examination. Because time is limited, you may also expect some rather abrupt switches in the direction the questioning takes, so do not be upset by it. Normally, a board member will not pursue a single line of questioning unless he discovers a particular strength or weakness.

After each member has participated, the chairman will usually ask whether any member has any further questions, then will ask you if you have anything you wish to add. Unless you are expecting this question, it may floor you. Worse, it may start you off on an extended, extemporaneous speech. The board is not usually seeking more information. The question is principally to offer you a last opportunity to present further qualifications or to indicate that you have nothing to add. So, if you feel that a significant qualification or characteristic has been overlooked, it is proper to point it out in a sentence or so. Do not compliment the board on the thoroughness of their examination – they have been sketchy, and you know it. If you wish, merely say, "No thank you, I have nothing further to add." This is a point where you can "talk yourself out" of a good impression or fail to present an important bit of information. Remember, *you close the interview yourself.*

The chairman will then say, "That is all, Mr. _____, thank you." Do not be startled; the interview is over, and quicker than you think. Thank him, gather your belongings and take your leave. Save your sigh of relief for the other side of the door.

How to put your best foot forward

Throughout this entire process, you may feel that the board individually and collectively is trying to pierce your defenses, seek out your hidden weaknesses and embarrass and confuse you. Actually, this is not true. They are obliged to make an appraisal of your qualifications for the job you are seeking, and they want to see you in your best light. Remember, they must interview all candidates and a non-cooperative candidate may become a failure in spite of their best efforts to bring out his qualifications. Here are 15 suggestions that will help you:

1) Be natural – Keep your attitude confident, not cocky

If you are not confident that you can do the job, do not expect the board to be. Do not apologize for your weaknesses, try to bring out your strong points. The board is interested in a positive, not negative, presentation. Cockiness will antagonize any board member and make him wonder if you are covering up a weakness by a false show of strength.

2) Get comfortable, but don't lounge or sprawl

Sit erectly but not stiffly. A careless posture may lead the board to conclude that you are careless in other things, or at least that you are not impressed by the importance of the occasion. Either conclusion is natural, even if incorrect. Do not fuss with your clothing, a pencil or an ashtray. Your hands may occasionally be useful to emphasize a point; do not let them become a point of distraction.

3) Do not wisecrack or make small talk

This is a serious situation, and your attitude should show that you consider it as such. Further, the time of the board is limited – they do not want to waste it, and neither should you.

4) Do not exaggerate your experience or abilities

In the first place, from information in the application or other interviews and sources, the board may know more about you than you think. Secondly, you probably will not get away with it. An experienced board is rather adept at spotting such a situation, so do not take the chance.

5) If you know a board member, do not make a point of it, yet do not hide it

Certainly you are not fooling him, and probably not the other members of the board. Do not try to take advantage of your acquaintanceship – it will probably do you little good.

6) Do not dominate the interview

Let the board do that. They will give you the clues – do not assume that you have to do all the talking. Realize that the board has a number of questions to ask you, and do not try to take up all the interview time by showing off your extensive knowledge of the answer to the first one.

7) Be attentive

You only have 20 minutes or so, and you should keep your attention at its sharpest throughout. When a member is addressing a problem or question to you, give him your undivided attention. Address your reply principally to him, but do not exclude the other board members.

8) Do not interrupt

A board member may be stating a problem for you to analyze. He will ask you a question when the time comes. Let him state the problem, and wait for the question.

9) Make sure you understand the question

Do not try to answer until you are sure what the question is. If it is not clear, restate it in your own words or ask the board member to clarify it for you. However, do not haggle about minor elements.

10) Reply promptly but not hastily

A common entry on oral board rating sheets is "candidate responded readily," or "candidate hesitated in replies." Respond as promptly and quickly as you can, but do not jump to a hasty, ill-considered answer.

11) Do not be peremptory in your answers

A brief answer is proper – but do not fire your answer back. That is a losing game from your point of view. The board member can probably ask questions much faster than you can answer them.

12) Do not try to create the answer you think the board member wants

He is interested in what kind of mind you have and how it works – not in playing games. Furthermore, he can usually spot this practice and will actually grade you down on it.

13) Do not switch sides in your reply merely to agree with a board member

Frequently, a member will take a contrary position merely to draw you out and to see if you are willing and able to defend your point of view. Do not start a debate, yet do not surrender a good position. If a position is worth taking, it is worth defending.

14) Do not be afraid to admit an error in judgment if you are shown to be wrong

The board knows that you are forced to reply without any opportunity for careful consideration. Your answer may be demonstrably wrong. If so, admit it and get on with the interview.

15) Do not dwell at length on your present job

The opening question may relate to your present assignment. Answer the question but do not go into an extended discussion. You are being examined for a *new* job, not your present one. As a matter of fact, try to phrase ALL your answers in terms of the job for which you are being examined.

Basis of Rating

Probably you will forget most of these "do's" and "don'ts" when you walk into the oral interview room. Even remembering them all will not ensure you a passing grade. Perhaps you did not have the qualifications in the first place. But remembering them will help you to put your best foot forward, without treading on the toes of the board members.

Rumor and popular opinion to the contrary notwithstanding, an oral board wants you to make the best appearance possible. They know you are under pressure – but they also want to see how you respond to it as a guide to what your reaction would be under the pressures of the job you seek. They will be influenced by the degree of poise you display, the personal traits you show and the manner in which you respond.

ABOUT THIS BOOK

This book contains tests divided into Examination Sections. Go through each test, answering every question in the margin. We have also attached a sample answer sheet at the back of the book that can be removed and used. At the end of each test look at the answer key and check your answers. On the ones you got wrong, look at the right answer choice and learn. Do not fill in the answers first. Do not memorize the questions and answers, but understand the answer and principles involved. On your test, the questions will likely be different from the samples. Questions are changed and new ones added. If you understand these past questions you should have success with any changes that arise. Tests may consist of several types of questions. We have additional books on each subject should more study be advisable or necessary for you. Finally, the more you study, the better prepared you will be. This book is intended to be the last thing you study before you walk into the examination room. Prior study of relevant texts is also recommended. NLC publishes some of these in our Fundamental Series. Knowledge and good sense are important factors in passing your exam. Good luck also helps. So now study this Passbook, absorb the material contained within and take that knowledge into the examination. Then do your best to pass that exam.

EXAMINATION SECTION

EXAMINATION SECTION
TEST 1

DIRECTIONS: Each question or incomplete statement is followed by several suggested answers or completions. Select the one that BEST answers the question or completes the statement. *PRINT THE LETTER OF THE CORRECT ANSWER IN THE SPACE AT THE RIGHT.*

Questions 1-5.

DIRECTIONS: Questions 1 through 5 are to be answered on the basis of the extracts from Federal income tax withholding and Social Security tax tables shown below. These tables indicate the amounts which must be withheld from the employee's salary by his employer for Federal income tax and for Social Security. They are based on weekly earnings.

| INCOME TAX WITHHOLDING TABLE ||||||||
| The wages are || And the number of withholding allowances is ||||||
At Least	But Less Than	5	6	7	8	9	10 or More
		The amount of income tax to be withheld shall be					
$300	$320	$24.60	$19.00	$13.80	$8.60	$4.00	$0
320	340	28.80	22.80	17.40	12.20	7.00	2.80
340	360	33.00	27.00	21.00	15.80	10.60	5.60
360	380	37.20	31.20	25.20	19.40	14.20	9.00
380	400	41.40	34.40	29.40	23.40	17.80	12.60
400	420	45.60	39.60	33.60	27.60	21.40	16.20
420	440	49.80	43.80	37.80	31.80	25.60	19.80
440	460	54.00	48.00	42.00	36.00	29.80	23.80
460	480	58.20	52.20	46.20	40.20	34.00	38.00
480	500	62.40	46.40	40.40	44.40	38.20	32.20

| SOCIAL SECURITY TABLE ||||||
| WAGES ||| WAGES |||
At Least	But Less Than	Tax to be Withheld	At Least	But Less Than	Tax to be Withheld
$333.18	$333.52	$19.50	$336.60	$336.94	$19.70
333.52	333.86	19.52	336.94	337.28	19.72
333.86	334.20	19.54	337.28	337.62	19.74
334.20	334.54	19.56	337.62	337.96	19.76
334.54	334.88	19.58	337.96	338.30	19.78
334.88	335.22	19.60	338.30	338.64	19.80
335.22	335.56	19.62	338.64	338.98	19.82
335.56	335.90	19.64	338.98	339.32	19.84
335.90	336.24	19.66	339.32	339.66	19.86
336.24	336.60	19.68	339.66	340.00	19.88

1. If an employee has a weekly wage of $379.50 and claims 6 withholding allowances, the amount of income tax to be withheld is
   A. $27.00   B. $31.20   C. $35.40   D. $37.20

2. An employee had wages of $335.60 for one week. With eight withholding allowances claimed, how much income tax will be withheld from his salary?
   A. $8.60   B. $12.00   C. $13.80   D. $17.40

3. How much social security tax will an employee with weekly wages of $335.60 pay?
   A. $19.60   B. $19.62   C. $19.64   D. $19.66

4. Mr. Wise earns $339.80 a week and claims seven withholding allowances. What is his take-home pay after income tax and social security tax are deducted?
   A. $300.32   B. $302.52   C. $319.92   D. $322.40

5. If an employee pays $19.74 in social security tax and claims eight withholding allowances, the amount of income tax that should be withheld from his wages is
   A. $8.60   B. $12.20   C. $13.80   D. $15.80

6. A fundamental rule of bookkeeping states that an individual's assets equal his liabilities plus his proprietorship (ASSETS = LIABILITIES – PROPRIETORSHIP). Which of the following statements logically follows from this rule?
   A. ASSETS = PROPRIETORSHIP – LIABILITIES
   B. LIABILITIES = ASSETS + PROPRIETORSHIP
   C. PROPRIETORSHIP = ASSETS – LIABILITIES
   D. PROPRIETORSHIP = LIABILITIES + ASSETS

7. Mr. Martin's assets consist of the following:
   Cash on Hand: $5,233.74
   Furniture: $4,925.00
   Government Bonds: $5,500.00
   What are his TOTAL assets?
   A. $10,158.74 $10,425.00   C. $10,733.74   D. $15,658.74

8. If Mr. Mitchell has $627.04 in his checking account and then writes three checks for $241.74, $13.24, and $101.97, what will be his new balance?
   A. $257.88   B. $269.08   C. $357.96   D. $368.96

9. An employee's net pay is equal to his total earnings less all deductions. If an employee's total earnings in a pay period are $497.05, what is his NET pay if he has the following deductions: Federal income tax, $90.32; FICA: $28.74; State tax: $18.79; City tax: $7.25; Pension: $1.88?
   A. $351.17   B. $351.07   C. $350.17   D. $350.07

10. A petty cash fund had an opening balance of $85.75 on December 1. 10.____
Expenditures of $23.00, $15.65, $5.23, $14.75, and $26.38 were made out of his fund during the first 14 days of the month. Then, on December 17, another $38.50 was added to the fund.
If additional expenditures of $17.18, $3.29, and $11.64 were made during the remainder of the month, what was the FINAL balance of the petty cash fund at the end of December?
   A. $6.93	B. $7.13	C. $46.51	D. $91.40

Questions 11-15.

DIRECTIONS: Questions 11 through 15 are to be answered on the basis of the following instructions.

The chart below is used by the loan division of a city retirement system for the following purposes: (1) to calculate the monthly payment a member must pay on an outstanding loan; (2) to calculate how much a member owes on an outstanding loan after he has made a number of payments.

To calculate the amount a member must pay each month in repaying his loan, look at Column II on the chart. You will notice that each entry in Column II corresponds to a number appearing under the *Months* column; for example, 1.004868 corresponds to 1 month, 0.503654 corresponds to 2 months, etc. To calculate the amount a member must pay each month, use the following procedure: multiply the amount of the load by the entry in Column II which corresponds to the number of months over which the load will be paid back. For example, if a loan of $200 is taken out for six months, multiply $200 by 0.169518, the entry in Column II which corresponds to six months.

In order to calculate the balance still owed on an outstanding loan, multiply the monthly payment by the number in Column I which corresponds to the number of monthly payments which remain to be paid on the loan. For example, if a member is supposed to pay $106.00 a month for twelve months, after seven payments, five monthly payments remain. To calculate the balance owed on the loan at this point, multiply the $106.00 monthly payment by 4.927807, the number in Column I that corresponds to five months.

Months	Column I	Column II
1	0.995156	1.004868
2	1.985491	0.503654
3	2.971029	0.336584
4	3.951793	0.253050
5	4.927807	0.202930
6	5.899092	0.169518
7	6.865673	0.145652
8	7.827572	0.127754
9	8.784811	0.113833
10	9.737414	0.102697
11	10.685402	0.093586
12	11.628798	0.085994
13	12.567624	0.079570
14	13.501902	0.074064
15	14.431655	0.069292

11. If Mr. Carson borrows $1,500 for eight months, how much will he have to pay back each month?
    A. $187.16   B. $191.63   C. $208.72   D. $218.65

11.____

12. If a member borrows $2,400 for one year, the amount he will have to pay back each month is
    A. $118.78   B. $196.18   C. $202.28   D. $206.38

12.____

13. Mr. Elliott borrowed $1,700 for a period of fifteen months. Each month he will have to pay back
    A. $117.80   B. $116.96   C. $107.79   D. $101.79

13.____

14. Mr. Aylward is paying back a thirteen-month loan at the rate of $173.13 a month.
    If he has already made six monthly payments, how much does he owe on the outstanding loan?
    A. $1,027.38   B. $1,178.75   C. $1,188.65   D. $1,898.85

14.____

15. A loan was taken out for 15 months, and the monthly payment was $104.75. After two monthly payments, how much was still owed on this load?
    A. $515.79   B. $863.89   C. $1,116.76   D. $1,316.46

15.____

16. The ABC Corporation had a gross income of $125,500.00 in 2015. Of this, it paid 60% for overhead.
    If the gross income for 2016 increased by $6,500 and the cost of overhead increased to 61% of gross income, how much more did it pay for overhead in 2016 than in 2015?
    A. $1,320   B. $5,220   C. $7,530   D. $8,052

16.____

17. After one year, Mr. Richards paid back a total of $1,695.00 as payment for 17.____
    a $1,500.00 loan. All the money paid over $1,500.00 was simple interest.
    The interest charge was MOST NEARLY
    A. 13%   B. 11%   C. 9%   D. 7%

18. A checking account has a balance of $253.36. 18.____
    If deposits of $36.95, $210.23, and $7.34 and withdrawals of $117.35, $23.37,
    and $15.98 are made, what is the NEW balance of the account?
    A. $155.54   B. $351.18   C. $364.58   D. $664.58

19. In 2015, the W Realty Company spent 27% of its income on rent. 19.____
    If it earned $97,254.00 in 2015, the amount it paid for rent was
    A. $26.258.58 B. $26,348.58 C. $27,248.58 D. $27,358.58

20. Six percent simple annual interest on $2,436.18 is MOST NEARLY 20.____
    A. $145.08   B. $145.17   c. $146.08   D. $146.17

21. Assume that the XYZ Company has $10,402.72 cash on hand. 21.____
    If it pays $699.83 of this for rent, the amount of cash on hand would be
    A. $9,792.89   B. $9,702.89   C. $9,692.89   D. $9,602.89

22. On January 31, Mr. Warren's checking account had a balance of $933.68. 22.____
    If he deposited $36.40 on February 2, $126.00 on February 9, and $90.02 on
    February 16 and wrote no checks during this period, what was the balance of his
    account on February 17?
    A. $680.26   B. $681.26   C. $1,186.10   D. $1,187.00

23. Multiplying a number by .75 is the same as 23.____
    A. multiplying it by 2/3   B. dividing it by 2/3
    C. multiplying it by 3/4   D. dividing it by 3/4

24. In City Agency A, 2/3 of the employees are enrolled in a retirement system. 24.____
    City Agency B has the same number of employees as Agency A, and 60% of
    these are enrolled in a retirement system.
    If Agency A has a total of 660 employees, how many MORE employees does it
    have enrolled in a retirement system than does Agency B?
    B. 36   B. 44   C. 56   D. 66

25. Net Worth is equal to Assets minus Liabilities. 25.____
    If, at the end of year, a textile company had assets of $98,695.83 and liabilities of
    $59,238.29, what was its net worth?
    A. $38,478.54 B. $38,488.64 C. $39,457.54 D. $48,557.54

KEY (CORRECT ANSWERS)

1.	B		11.	B
2.	B		12.	D
3.	C		13.	A
4.	B		14.	C
5.	B		15.	D
6.	C		16.	B
7.	D		17.	A
8.	B		18.	B
9.	D		19.	A
10.	B		20.	D

21. B
22. C
23. C
24. B
25. C

TEST 2

DIRECTIONS: Each question or incomplete statement is followed by several suggested answers or completions. Select the one that BEST answers the question or completes the statement. *PRINT THE LETTER OF THE CORRECT ANSWER IN THE SPACE AT THE RIGHT.*

Questions 1-10.

DIRECTIONS: Questions 1 through 10 below present the identification numbers, initials, and last names of employees enrolled in a city retirement system. You are to choose the option (A, B, C, or D) that has the IDENTICAL identification number, initials, and last name as those given in each question.

<u>Sample Question</u>
B145698 JL Jones
    A.   B146798 JL Jones
    C.   P145698 JL Jones
    B.   B145698 JL Jonas
    D.   B145698 JL Jones

    The correct answer is D. Only Option D shows the identification number, initials, and last name exactly as they are in the sample question. Options A, B, and C have errors in the identification number or last name.

1. J297483 PL Robinson
   A. J294783 PL Robinson
   C. J297483 Pl Robinson
   B. J297483 PL Robinson
   D. J297843 PL Robinson

1.____

2. S497662 JG Schwartz
   B. S497662 JG Schwarz
   C. S497662 JG Schwartz
   B. S497762 JG Schwartz
   D. S497663 JG Schwartz

2.____

3. G696436 LN Alberton
   A. G696436 LM Alberton
   C. G696346 LN Albertson
   B. G696436 LN Albertson
   D. G696436 LN Alberton

3.____

4. R774923 AD Aldrich
   A. R774923 AD Aldrich
   C. R774932 AP Aldrich
   B. R744923 AD Aldrich
   D. R774932 AD Allrich

4.____

5. N239638 RP Hrynyk
   A. N236938 PR Hrynyk
   C. N239638 PR Hrynyk
   B. N236938 RP Hrynyk
   D. N239638 Hrynyk

5.____

6. R156949 LT Carlson
   A. R156949 LT Carlton
   C. R159649 LT Carlton
   B. R156494 LT Carlson
   D. R156949 LT Carlson

6.____

7. T524697 MN Orenstein
   A. T524697 MN Orenstein
   C. T524697 NM Ornstein
   B. T524967 MN Orinstein
   D. T524967 NM Orenstein

7.____

8. L346239 JD Remsen
   A. L346239 JD Remson
   B. L364239 JD Remsen
   C. L346329 JD Remsen
   D. L346239 JD Remsen

   8._____

9. P966438 SB Rieperson
   A. P996438 SB Rieperson
   B. P466438 SB Reiperson
   C. R996438 SB Rieperson
   D. P966438 SB Rieperson

   9._____

10. D749382 CD Thompson
    A. P749382 CD Thompson
    B. D749832 CD Thomsonn
    C. D749382 CD Thompson
    D. D749823 CD Thomspon

    10._____

Questions 11-20.

DIRECTIONS: Assume that each of the capital letters in the table below represents the name of an employee enrolled in the city's employees' personnel system. The number directly beneath the letter represents the agency for which the employee works, and the small letter directly beneath represents the code for the employee's account.

Name of Employee	L	O	T	Q	A	M	R	N	C
Agency	3	4	5	9	8	7	2	1	6
Account Code	r	f	b	i	d	t	g	e	n

In each of the following Questions 11 through 20, the agency code numbers and the account code letters in Columns 2 and 3 should correspond to the capital letters in Column 1 and should be in the same consecutive order. For each question, look at each column carefully and mark your answer as follows:

If there are one or more errors in Column 2 only, mark your answer A.
If there are one or more errors in Column 3 only, mark your answer B.
I there are one or more errors in Column 2 and one or more errors in Column 3, mark your answer C.
If there are NO errors in either column, mark your answer D.

Sample Question

Column 1	Column 2	Column 3
TQLMOC	583746	birtfn

In Column 2, the second agency code number (corresponding to letter Q) should be 9, not 8. Column 3 is coded correctly to Column 1. Since there is an error only in Column 2, the correct answer is A.

	COLUMN 1	COLUMN 2	COLUMN 3	
11.	QLNRCA	931268	iregnd	11._____
12.	NRMOTC	127546	egftbn	12._____
13.	RCTALM	265837	gndbrt	13._____
14.	TAMLON	578341	bdtrfe	14._____
15.	ANTORM	815427	debigt	15._____
16.	MRALON	728341	tgdrfe	16._____
17.	CTNQRO	657924	ndeigf	17._____
18.	QMROTA	972458	itgfbd	18._____
19.	RQMCOL	297463	gitnfr	19._____
20.	NOMRTQ	147259	eftgbi	20._____

Questions 21-25.

DIRECTIONS: Questions 21 through 25 are to be answered SOLELY on the basis of the following passage.

The city may issue its own bonds or it may purchase bonds as an investment. Bonds may be issued in various denominations, and the face value of the bond is its par value. Before purchasing a bond, the investor desires to know the rate of income that the investment may yield in computing the yield on a bond, it is assumed that the investor will keep the bond until the date of maturity, except for callable bonds which are not considered in this passage. To compute exact yield is a complicated mathematical problem, and scientifically prepared tables are generally used to avoid such computation. However, the approximate yield can be computed much more easily. In computing approximate yield, the accrued interest on the date of purchase should be ignored because the buyer who pays accrued interest to the seller receives it again at the next interest date. Bonds bought at a premium (which cost more) yield a lower rate of income than the same bonds bought at par (face value), and bounds bought at a discount (which cost less) yield a higher rate of income than the same bonds bought at par.

21. An investor bought a $10,000 city bond paying 6% interest. 21._____
    Which of the following purchase prices would indicate that the bond was
    bought at a premlum?
    A. $9,000   B. $9,400   C. $10,000   D. $10,600

22. During 2016, a particular $10,000 bond paying 7 ½% sold at fluctuating prices. 22._____
    Which of the following prices would indicate that the bond was bought at a
    discount?
    A. $9,800   B. $10,000   C. $10,200   D. $10,750

23. A certain group of bonds was sold in denominations of $5,000, $10,000, $20,000, and $50,000.
In the following list of four purchase prices, which one is MOST likely to represent a bond sold at par value?
A. $10,500   B. $20,000   C. $22,000   D. $49,000

23._____

24. When computing the approximate yield on a bond, it is DESIRABLE to
A. assume the bond was purchased at par
B. consult scientifically prepared tables
C. ignore accrued interest on the date of purchase
D. wait until the bond reaches maturity

24._____

25. Which of the following is MOST likely to be an exception to the information provided in the above passage?
Bonds
A. purchased at a premium
B. sold at par
C. sold before maturity
D. which are callable

25._____

KEY (CORRECT ANSWERS)

1.	B		11.	D
2.	C		12.	C
3.	D		13.	B
4.	A		14.	A
5.	D		15.	B
6.	D		16.	D
7.	A		17.	C
8.	D		18.	D
9.	D		19.	A
10.	C		20.	D

21. D
22. A
23. B
24. C
25. D

TEST 3

DIRECTIONS: Each question or incomplete statement is followed by several suggested answers or completions. Select the one that BEST answers the question or completes the statement. *PRINT THE LETTER OF THE CORRECT ANSWER IN THE SPACE AT THE RIGHT.*

Questions 1-6.

DIRECTIONS: Questions 1 through 6 consist of computations of addition, subtraction, multiplication, and division. For each question, do the computation indicated, and choose the correct answer from the four choices given.

1. ADD: 8936
   7821
   8953
   4297
   9785
   6579

   A. 45371   B. 45381   C. 46371   D. 46381

   1.____

2. SUBTRACT: 95,432
   67,596

   A. 27,836   B. 27,846   C. 27,936   D. 27,946

   2.____

3. MULTIPLY: 987
   867

   A. 854609   B. 854729   C. 855709   D. 855729

   3.____

4. DIVIDE: 59)321439.0

   A. 5438.1   B. 5447.1   C. 5448.1   D. 5457.1

   4.____

5. DIVIDE: .057)721

   A. 12,648.0   B. 12,648.1   C. 12,649.0   D. 12,649.1

   5.____

6. ADD: 1/2 + 5/7
   A. 1 3/14   B. 1 2/7   C. 1 5/14   D. 1 3/7

   6.____

7. If the total number of employees in one city agency increased from 1,927 to 2,006 during a certain year, the percentage increase in the number of employees for that year is MOST NEARLY
   A. 4%   B. 5%   C. 6%   D. 7%

   7.____

8. During a single fiscal year, which totaled 248 workdays, one account clerk verified 1,488 purchase vouchers.
   Assuming a normal work week of five days, what is the average number of vouchers verified by the account clerk in a one-week period during this fiscal year?
   A. 25   B. 30   C. 35   D. 40

9. If the city department of purchase bought 190 computers for $793.50 each and 208 computers for $839.90 each, the TOTAL price paid for these computers is
   A. $315,813.00
   B. $325,464.20
   C. $334,279.20
   D. $335,863.00

Questions 10-14.

DIRECTIONS: Questions 10 through 14 are to be answered SOLELY on the basis of the information given in the following paragraph.

Since discounts are in common use in the commercial world and apply to purchases made by government agencies as well as business firms, it is essential that individuals in both public and private employment who prepare bills, check invoices, prepare payment vouchers, or write checks to pay bills have an understanding of the terms used. These include cash or time discount, trade discount, and disconnect series. A cash or time discount offers a reduction in price to the buyer for the prompt payment of the bill and is usually expressed as a percentage with a time requirement, stated in days, within which the bill must be paid in order to earn the discount. An example would be 3/10, meaning a 3% discount may be applied to the bill if the payment is forwarded to the vendor within ten days. On an invoice, the cash discount terms are usually followed by the net terms, which is the time in days allowed for ordinary payment of the bill. Thus, 3/10, Net 30 means that full payment is expected in thirty days if the cash discount of 3% is not taken for having paid the bill within ten days. When the expression Terms Net Cash is listed on a bill, it means that no deduction for early payment is allowed. A trade discount is normally applied to list prices by a manufacturer to show the actual price to retailers so that they may know their cost and determine markups that will allow them to operate competitively and at a profit. A trade discount is applied by the seller to the list price and is independent of a cash or time discount. Discounts may also be used by manufacturers to adjust prices charged to retailers without changing list prices. This is usually done by series discounting and is expressed as a series of percentages. To compute a series discount, such as 40%, 20%, 10%, first apply the 40% discount to the list price, then apply the 20% discount to the remainder, and finally apply the 10% discount to the second remainder.

10. According to the above passage, trade discounts are
    A. applied by the buyer
    B. independent of cash discounts
    C. restricted to cash sales
    D. used to secure rapid payment of bills

11. According to the above passage, if the sales terms 5/10, Net 60 appear on a bill in the amount of $100 dated December 5, 2016 and the buyer submits his payment on December 15, 2016, his PROPER payment should be
    A. $60   B. $90   C. $95   D. $100

12. According to the above passage, if a manufacturer gives a trade discount of 40% for an item with a list price of $250 and the terms are Net Cash, the price a retail merchant is required to pay for this item is   12.____
    A. $250   B. $210   C. $150   D. $100

13. According to the above passage, a series discount of 25%, 20%, 10% applied to a list price of $200 results in an ACTUAL price to the buyer of   13.____
    A. $88   B. $90   C. $108   D. $110

14. According to the above passage, if a manufacturer gives a trade discount of 50% and the terms are 6/10, Net 30, the cost to a retail merchant of an item with a list price of $500 and for which he takes the time discount is   14.____
    A. $220   B. $235   C. $240   D. $250

Questions 15-22.

DIRECTIONS: Questions 15 through 22 each show in Column I the information written on five cards (lettered j, k, l, m, n) which have to be filed. You are to choose the option (lettered A, B, C, or D) in Column II which BEST represents the proper order of filing according to the information, rules, and sample question given below.

A file card record is kept of the work assignments for all the employees in a certain bureau. On each card is the employee's name, the date of work assignment, and the work assignment code number. The cards are to be filed according to the following rules:

FIRST: File in alphabetical order according to employee's name.

SECOND: When two or more cards have the same employee's name, file according to the assignment date, beginning with the earliest date.

THIRD: When two or more cards have the same employee's name and the same date, file according to the work assignment number beginning with the lowest number.

Column II shows the cards arranged in four different orders. Pick the option (A, B, C, or D) in Column II which shows the correct arrangement of the cards according to th above filing rules.

SAMPLE QUESTION

Column I
j. Cluney 4/8/02 (486503)
k. Roster 5/10/01 (246611)
l. Altool 10/15/02 (711433)
m. Cluney 12/18/02 (527610)
n. Cluney 4/8/02 (486500)

Column II
A. k, l, m, j, n
B. k, n, j, l, m
C. l, k, j, m, n
D. l, n, j, m, k

4 (#3)

The correct way to file the cards is:
  l. Altool 10/15/02 (71143)
  n. Cluney 4/8/02 (486500)
  j. Cluney 4/8/02 (486503)
  m. Cluney 12/18/02 (527610)
  k. Roster 5/10/01 (246611)

The correct filing order is shown by the letters l, n, j, m, k. The answer to the sample question is the letter D, which appears in front of the letters l, n, j, m, k in Column II.

COLUMN I	COLUMN II	
15. j. Smith 3/19/03 (662118) k. Turner 4/16/99 (481349) l. Terman 3/20/02 (210229) m. Smyth 3/20/02 (481359) n. Terry 5/11/01 (672128)	A. j, m, l, n, k B. j, l, n, m, k C. k, n, m, l, j D. j, n, k, l, m	15.____
16. j. Ross 5/29/02 (396118) k. Rosner 5/29/02 (439281) l. Rose 7/19/02 (723456) m. Rosen 5/29/03 (829692) n. Ross 5/29/02 (399118)	A. l, m, k, n, j B. m, l, k, n, j C. l, m, k, j, n D. m, l, j, n, k	16.____
17. j. Sherd 10/12/99 (552368) k. Snyder 11/12/99 (539286) l. Shindler 10/13/98 (426798) m. Scherld 10/12/99 (552386) n. Schneider 11/12/99 (798213)	A. n, m, k, j, l B. j, m, l, k, n C. m, k, n, j. l D. m, n, j, l, k	17.____
18. j. Carter 1/16/02 (489636) k. Carson 2/16/01 (392671) l. Carter 1/16/01 (486936) m. Carton 3/15/00 (489639) n. Carson 2/16/01 (392617)	A. k, n, j, l, m B. n, k, m, l, j C. n, k, l, j, m D. k, n, l, j, m	18.____
19. j. Thomas 3/18/99 (763182) k. Tompkins 3/19/00 (928439) l. Thomson 3/21/00 (763812) m. Thompson 3/18/99 (924893) n. Tompson 3/19/99 (928793)	A. m, l, j, k, n B. j, m, l, k, n C. j, l, n, m, k D. l, m, j, n, k	19.____
20. j. Breit 8/10/03 (345612) k. Briet 5/21/00 (837543) l. Bright 9/18/99 (931827) m. Breit 3/7/98 (553984) n. Brent 6/14/04 (682731)	A. m, j, n, k, l B. n, m, j, k, l C. m, j, k, l, n D. j, m, k, l, n	20.____

COLUMN I   COLUMN II

21. j. Roberts 10/19/02 (581932)   A. n, k, l, m, j   21._____
     k. Rogers 8/9/00 (638763)   B. n, k, l, j, m
     l. Rogerts 7/15/97 (105689)   C. k, n, l, m, j
     m. Robin 3/8/92 (287915)   D. j, m, k, n, l
     n. Rogers 4/2/04 (736921)

22. j. Hebert 4/28/02 (719468)   A. n, k, j, m, l   22._____
     k. Herbert 5/8/01 (938432)   B. j, l, n, k, m
     l. Helbert 9/23/04 (832912)   C. l, j, k, n, m
     m. Herbst 7/10/03 (648599)   D. l, j, n, k, m
     n. Herbert 5/8/01 (487627)

23. In order to pay its employees, the Convex Company obtained bills and coins   23._____
    in the following denominations:

Denomination	$20	$10	$5	$1	$.50	$.25	$.10	$.05	$.01
Number	317	122	38	73	69	47	39	25	36

    What was the TOTAL amount of cash obtained?
    A. $7,874.76   B. $7,878.00   C. $7,889.25   D. $7,924.35

24. H. Partridge receives a weekly gross salary (before deductions) of $596.25.   24._____
    Through weekly payroll deductions of $19.77, he is paying back a load he took
    from his pension fund.
    If other fixed weekly deductions amount to $184.14, how much pay would Mr.
    Partridge take home over a period of 33 weeks?
    A. $11,446.92   B. $12,375.69   C. $12,947.22   D. $19,676.25

25. Mr. Robertson is a city employee enrolled in a city retirement system. He has   25._____
    taken out a loan from the retirement fund and is paying it back at the rate of
    $14.90 every two weeks.
    In eighteen weeks, how much money will he have paid back on the loan?
    A. $268.20   B. $152.80   C. $124.10   D. $67.05

26. In 2015, the Iridor Book Company had the following expenses: rent, $6,500;   26._____
    overhead, $52,585; inventory, $35,700; and miscellaneous, $1,275.
    If all of these expenses went up 18% in 2016, what would they TOTAL in 2016?
    A. $17,290.80   B. $78,768.20   C. $96,060.00   D. $113,350.80

27. Ms. Ranier had a gross salary of $355.36, paid once every week.   27._____
    If the deductions from each paycheck are $62.72, $25.13, $6.29, and $1,27, how
    much money would Ms. Ranier take home in four weeks?
    A. $1,039.80   B. $1,421.44   C. $2,079.60   D. $2,842.88

28. Mr. Martin had a net income of $19,100 for the year. 28.____
If he spent 34% on rent and household expenses, 3% on house furnishings, 25% on clothes, and 36% on food, how much was left for savings and other expenses?
   A. $196.00   B. $382.00   C. $649.40   D. $1,960.00

29. Mr. Elsberg can pay back a loan of $1,800 from the city employees' retirement 29.____
system if he pays back $36.69 every two weeks for two full years.
At the end of the two years, how much more than the original $1,800 he borrowed will Mr. Elsberg have paid back?
   A. $53.94   B. $107.88   C. $190.79   D. $214.76

30. Mrs. Nusbaum is a city employee, receiving a gross salary (salary before 30.____
deductions) of $31,200. Every two weeks, the following deductions are taken out of her salary: Federal Income Tax, $243.96; FICA, $66.39; State Tax, $44.58; City Tax, $20.91; Health Insurance, $4.71.
If Mrs. Nusbaum's salary and deductions remained the same for a full calendar year, what would her NET salary (gross salary less deductions) be in that year?
   A. $9,894.30   B. $21,305.70   C. $28,118.25   D. $30,819.45

KEY (CORRECT ANSWERS)

1.	C	11.	C	21.	D
2.	A	12.	C	22.	B
3.	D	13.	C	33.	A
4.	C	14.	B	24.	C
5.	D	15.	A	25.	C
6.	A	16.	C	26.	D
7.	A	17.	D	27.	A
8.	B	18.	C	28.	B
9.	B	19.	B	29.	B
10.	B	20.	A	30.	B

ARITHMETIC

EXAMINATION SECTION

TEST 1

DIRECTIONS: Each question or incomplete statement is followed by several suggested answers or completions. Select the one that BEST answers the question or completes the statement. *PRINT THE LETTER OF THE CORRECT ANSWER IN THE SPACE AT THE RIGHT.*

1. 575 × 269 =
   A. 156,475   B. 154,765   C. 154,675   D. none of the above   1.____

2. 837 × 720 =
   A. 602,640   B. 602,460   C. 620,460   D. none of the above   2.____

3. 414 × 961 =
   A. 397,854   B. 397,845   C. 397,485   D. none of the above   3.____

4. 898 × 303 =
   A. 272,049   B. 272,904   C. 272,194   D. none of the above   4.____

5. 5,623 × 2,183 =
   A. 12,275,099   B. 12,275,009   C. 12,276,009   D. none of the above   5.____

6. 913.67 × 1.04 =
   A. 950.1628   B. 9502.168   C. 950.2168   D. none of the above   6.____

7. 313 × 2.78 =
   A. 860.41   B. 870.13   C. 870.10   D. none of the above   7.____

8.
   ```
    69
    23
    12
   +14
   ```
   A. 117   B. 118   C. 120   D. none of the above   8.____

9.
   ```
   318
   902
    45
   +18
   ```
   A. 1,228   B. 1,282   C. 1,828   D. none of the above   9.____

10. $78.50
      .65
     18.20
     +7.07

    A. $204.42   B. $214.43   C. $214.42   D. none of the above

11. 8.6809
     .7516
     +1.5403

    A. 10.9787   B. 10.9738   C. 10.9728   D. none of the above

12. 53
     781
     60
     199

    A. 1,003   B. 1,099   C. 1,093   D. none of the above

13. 6 1/8
     4 2/3
     +9 1/6

    A. 19 23/24   B. 20 11/12   C. 19 21/24   D. none of the above

14. 2 1/2
     8 1/4
     +7 1/6

    A. 17 5/6   B. 17 11/13   C. 18 1/12   D. none of the above

15. $463.57
     - 84.68

    A. $378.88   B. $388.89   C. $378.89   D. none of the above

16. $1,682.40
     -   834.12

    A. $848.82   B. $848.22   C. $884.28   D. none of the above

17. 991.17
     -916.68

    A. 74.99   B. 74.49   C. 79.99   D. none of the above

3 (#1)

18. 6,241
    - 861

    A. 5,480   B. 5,380   C. 5,408   D. none of the above

    18.____

19. 8971.6
    - 333.3

    A. 8648.3   B. 8638.3   C. 8683.3   D. none of the above

    19.____

20. 39 1/4
    - 7 1/2

    A. 31 1/2   B. 31 3/4   C. 30 1/2   D. none of the above

    20.____

21. $6\sqrt{5052}$ =
    A. 842   B. 804   C. 844   D. none of the above

    21.____

22. $12\sqrt{7596}$ =
    A. 630   B. 603   C. 636   D. none of the above

    22.____

23. $14\sqrt{368.501}$ =
    A. 26.3251   B. 25.3255   C. 26.3215   D. none of the above

    23.____

24. $21\sqrt{391.73}$ =
    A. 18.654 (approximately)   B. 18653 (approximately)
    C. 18.635 (approximately)   D. none of the above

    24.____

25. $5.4\sqrt{175.5}$ =
    A. 325.4   B. 32.45   C. 33.55   D. none of the above

    25.____

26. $2\sqrt{8\ 3/8}$ =
    A. 4 7/16   B. 4 3/4   C. 4 3/16   D. none of the above

    26.____

27. $6\sqrt{25\ 4/5}$ =
    A. 4 3/10   B. 4/25   C. 4 1/3   D. none of the above

    27.____

28. Change the following to decimal form $\frac{15}{14}$
    A. .652   B. .655   C. .625   D. none of the above

    28.____

29. Take 1/6 of 372
    A. 57   B. 48   C. 62   D. none of the above

    29.____

30. Take 1/11 of 380.6
    A. 36.4   B. 34.6   C. 36.6   D. none of the above

    30.____

31. Find 7 1/2% of $3,600
    A. $280 B. $270 C. $275 D. none of the above

32. Find 16% of $215
    A. $34.40 B. $33.44 C. $34.04 D. none of the above

33. Find 9 3/4% of 14
    A. 1.365 B. 1.356 C. 1,565 D. none of the above

34. Find 3 4/5% of 15.5
    A. .597 B. .589 C. .579 D. none of the above

35. Find 28% of $6535
    A. $1789.40 B. $1839.40 C. $1788.49 D. none of the above

36. If .25 is divided by 40, the result is
    A. .00625 B. .0625 C. .625 D. none of the above

37. The number 40 is 80% of
    A. 45 B. 50 C. 55 D. none of the above

38. The number 24 is 60% of
    A. 30 B. 35 C. 40 D. none of the above

39. If 9/10 of a number is 54, the number is
    A. 63 B. 60 C. 74 D. none of the above

40. If 4/7 of a number is 64, the number is
    A. 122 B. 108 C. 112 D. none of the above

41. If 45 is divided by .15, the result is
    A. 30 B. 300 c. 3000 D. none of the above

42. If 29,021.251 is divided by 61.879, the result is
    A. 4690 B. 469 C. 405 D. none of the above

43. If 5,252.52 is divided by 62.53, the result is
    A. 84 B. 790 C. 79 D. none of the above

44. If 20% of a number is 62, the number is
    A. 295 B. 305 C. 334 D. none of the above

45. If 55% of a number is 220, the number is
    A. 405 B. 400 C. 380 D. none of the above

46. If the product of 160 multiplied by .06 is subtracted from the product of 17.5 multiplied by .7, the result is
    A. 2.65 B. 3.2 C. 4.1 D. none of the above

47. Add the following lengths: 3 feet, 2 inches; 4 yards, 8 inches; 6 yards, 10 feet, 3 inches; 8 feet 2 inches; and give the answer in feet and fractions thereof.
    A. 52 ¼'   B. 52 1/3'   C. 53 1/4'   D. none of the above

48. What is the net amount of a bill of $354 after a discount of 12% has been allowed?
    A. $311.25   B. $311.52   C. $312.52   D. none of the above

49. What is the net amount of a bill of $675.50 after a discount of 9% has been allowed?
    A. $641.07   B. $614.07   C. $614.70   D. none of the above

50. At 6 cents each, the cost of 215 plastic forks would be
    A. $15.06   B. $18.60   C. $21.86   D. none of the above

51. The sum of the numbers 46,385, 54,672, 6,210, 4,527, 38,925 is
    A. 150,917   B. 150,719   C. 170,919   D. none of the above

52. The sum of the numbers 462, 75,832, 6,731, 60,235, 8,427 is
    A. 143,463   B. 154,687   C. 174,823   D. none of the above

53. If a log measuring 8 feet, 4 inches is divided into five equal parts, each part is
    A. 1 foot
    B. 1 foot, 1 3/4 inches
    C. 1 foot, 4 1/3 inches
    D. none of the above

54. If erasers are sold at the rate of 5 for 18 cents, then 45 erasers will cost
    A. $1.62   B. $1.72   C. $1.82   D. none of the above

55. If erasers are sold at the rate of 4 for 6 cents, then 120 erasers will cost
    A. $1.65   B. $1.75   C. $1.85   D. none of the above

KEY (CORRECT ANSWERS)

1. C	11. C	21. A	31. B	41. B	51. B
2. A	12. C	22. D	32. A	42. B	52. B
3. A	13. A	23. C	33. A	43. A	53. D
4. D	14. D	24. A	34. B	44. D	54. A
5. B	15. C	25. D	35. D	45. B	55. D
6. C	16. D	26. C	36. A	46. A	
7. B	17. A	27. A	37. B	47. A	
8. B	18. B	28. C	38. C	48. B	
9. D	19. B	29. C	39. B	49. C	
10. A	20. B	30. B	40. C	50. D	

6 (#1)

SOLUTIONS TO PROBLEMS

1. (575)(269) = 154M675

2. (837)(720) = 602,640

3. (414)(962) = 397,854

4. (898)(304) = 272,094

5. (5623×2183) = 12,275,009

6. (913,67×1.04(= 950.2168

7. (313)(2.78) = 870,14

8. 69 + 23 + 12 + 14 = 117

9. 318 + 902 + 45 + 18 = 1283

10. $78.50 + .65 + $118.20 + $7.07 = 204.42

11. 8.6809 + .7516 + 1.5403 = 10.9728

12. 53 + 781 + 60 + 199 = 10.9728

13. 6 1/8 + 4 2/3 + 9 1/6 = 6 3/24 + 4 16/24 + 9 4/24 = 19 23/24

14. 2 ½ + 8 1/4 + 7 1/6 = 2 6/12 + 8 3/12 + 7 2/12 = 17 11/12

15. $463.57 - $84.68 = $378.89

16. $1682.49 - $834.12 = $848.28

17. 991.17 – 916.18 = 74.99

18. 6241 – 861 = 5380

19. 8971.6 – 333.3 = 8638.3

20. 39 1/4 – 7 1/2 = 39 1/4 – 7 2/4 = 31 3/4

21. 5052 ÷ 6 = 842

22. 7596 ÷ 12 = 633

23. 368.501 ÷ 14 = 26.3215

7 (#1)

24. 391.73 ÷ 21 ≈ 18.654

25. 175.5 ÷ 5.4 ≈ 32.5

26. $8(\frac{3}{4}) \div 2 = (\frac{67}{8})(\frac{1}{2}) = \frac{67}{16} = 4\frac{3}{16}$

27. $25(\frac{4}{5}) \div 6 = (\frac{129}{5})(\frac{1}{6}) = (\frac{129}{30}) = 4\frac{3}{10}$

28. 15/24 = .625

29. (1/6)(372) = 62

30. (1/11)(380.6) = 34.6

31. (.075)($3600) = $270

32. (.16)($215) = $34.40

33. $9\frac{3}{4}$% of 14 = (.0975)(14) = 1.365

34. 3 4/5% of 15.5 = (.038)(15.5) = .589

35. (.28)($6535) = $1829.80

36. .25÷40 = .00625

37. 40 = 80% of x. Then, x = 40 ÷ 80 = 50

38. 24 = 60% of x. Then, x = 24 ÷ 60 = 40

39. 9/10 of x = 54. Then, x = 54 ÷ 9/10 = 60

40. 4/7 of x = 65. Then, x = 64 ÷ 4/7 = 112

41. 45 ÷ .15 = 300

42. 29,021.251 ÷ 61.879 = 469

43. 5252.52 ÷ 62.53 = 84

44. 20% of x = 62. Then, x = 62 ÷ .20 = 310

45. 55% of x = 220. Then, x = 220 ÷ .55 = 400

46. (17.5)(.7) − (160)(.06) = 12.25 − 9.6 = 2.65

8 (#1)

47. 3 ft. 2 in. + 4 yds, 8 in. + 6 yds. 10 ft. 3 in. + 8 ft. 2 in. = 3 ft. 2 in. + 12 ft. 8 in. + 28 ft. 3 in. + 8 ft. 2 in. = 51 ft. 15 in. = 52 ft. 3 in. = 52 1/4 ft.

48. $354 – (.12)($354) = $354 - $42.48 = $311.52

49. $675.50 – (.09)($675.50) ≈ $675.50 - $60.80 = $614.70

50. (215)(.06) = $12.90

51. 46,385 + 54,672 + 6210 + 4527 + 38,925 = 150,719

52. 462 + 75,832 + 6731 + 60,235 + 8427 = 151,687

53. 8 ft. 4 in. ÷ 5 = 100 in. ÷ 5 = 20 in. = 1 ft. 8 in.

54. Let x = cost. Then, 5/.18 = 45/x, 5x = 8.10, x = $1.62

55. Let x = cost. Then, 4/.06 = 120/x , 4x = 7.20, x = $1.80

ARITHMETIC
EXAMINATION SECTION
TEST 1

DIRECTIONS: Each question or incomplete statement is followed by several suggested answers or completions. Select the one that BEST answers the question or completes the statement. *PRINT THE LETTER OF THE CORRECT ANSWER IN THE SPACE AT THE RIGHT.*

1. 34)17136   1.____

    A. 54   B. 503 24/34   C. 504
    D. 505 4/34   E. NG

2. 141606
   -94679   2.____

    A. 46,837   B. 46,927   C. 46,937   D. 47,027   E. NG

3. 86)8642   3.____

    A. 96   B. 96 76/86   C. 97 6/86
    D. 97 16/86   E. NG

4. $1\frac{2}{3}$
   $+1\frac{5}{6}$ 4.____

    A. 2 1/6   B. 2 1/2   C. 3 1/2   D. 3 1/3   E. NG

5. 3)128.94   5.____

    A. 42.98   B. 4.298   C. 429.8   D. 4298   E. NG

6. 709
   ×864   6.____

    A. 612,576   B. 602,576   C. 611,576
    D. 612,566   E. NG

7. 138057
   -54368   7.____

    A. 83,679   B. 83,689   C. 83,789   D. 84,689   E. NG

2 (#1)

8. $3\frac{3}{5} \div \frac{9}{10} =$

   A. 1/4   B. 2 1/2   C. 2 3/5   D. 3 3/5   E. NG

9. 7)21.442

   A. 3.063   B. 3.63   C. .363   D. 3063   E. NG

10. $\frac{9}{10} \cdot \frac{1}{2} =$

   A. 3/5   B. 2/5   C. 1/2   D. 1 2/5   E. NG

11. $\frac{2}{3} \times 2\frac{1}{4} =$

   A. 1   B. 2 1/2   C. 2   D. 1 1/2   E. NG

12. 7646
     6799
     3389
    +6597

   A. 23,431   B. 24,331   C. 24,431   D. 24,421   E. NG

13. $\frac{5}{6}$
    +$1\frac{3}{4}$

   A. 2 7/12   B. 1 4/5   C. 1 1/12   D. 2 ½   E. NG

14. Round to tenths: 22.3 – 1.21 =

   A. 21.0   B. 21.5   C. 21.8   D. 21.9   E. NG

15. Round to 2 digits: 9.05
                        ×5.9

   A. 53   B. 5.4   C. 5.3   D. 54   E. NG

16. 608
    ×970

   A. 58,776   B. 58,876   C. 588,760   D. 589,760   E. NG

17. 6567
     8999
     6877
    +8789

   A. 30,232   B. 31,132   C. 31,222   D. 31,232   E. NG

18. 4987
    × 96

   A. 468,752   B. 477,752   C. 478,742   D. 478,752   E. NG

19. $3\frac{1}{3}$
    $-1\frac{3}{4}$

   A. 1 5/12   B. 1 7/12   C. 2 1/2   D. 2 7/2   E. NG

20. What is 4% of $500?
   A. $20.00   B. $1.25   C. $2.00   D. $80.00   E. NG

21. 16
    ×$10\frac{3}{4}$

   A. 160   B. 160 3/4   C. 167 1/2   D. 172   E. NG

22. If $\frac{16}{K}$ = 8, then K =

   A. 1/2   B. 8   C. 128   D. 2   E. NG

23. Round to tenths:
    4.35
    ×0.32

   A. 1.3   B. 13.9   C. 1.4   D. 14.0   E. NG

24. What is $2\frac{1}{2}$% of $50?

   A. $12.50   B. $1.25   C. $25.00   D. $125.00   E. NG

25. 89)6267.38

   A. 7.42   B. 74.2   C. 7042   D. 70.42   E. NG

26. $10 is what percent of $400?
   A. 4   B. 25   C. 2 1/2   D. 40   E. NG

27. $.68\overline{)31.96}$
    A. 0.47   B. 47   C. 4.7   D. 470   E. NG   27.____

28. $\frac{4}{6} = \frac{N}{24}$
    A. 6   B. 18   C. 16   D. 36   E. NG   28.____

29. 6÷10 =
    A. 2/3   B. 3/5   C. 1 2/3   D. 6   E. NG   29.____

30. $\frac{3}{10} = \frac{15}{N}$
    A. 5   B. 40   C. 45   D. 150   E. NG   30.____

31. $\frac{3a}{4} = 6$
    a =
    A. 2   B. 24   C. 8   D. 72   E. NG   31.____

32. $40 is what percent of $1600?
    A. 20   B. 6.40   C. 2 1/2   D. 40   E. NG   32.____

33. $25 is 5% of what amount?
    A. $1.25   B. $125.00   C. $5000.00   D. $500.00   E. NG   33.____

34. (-3)
    ×6
    A. 9   B. 15   C. 18   D. -18   E. NG   34.____

35. $160 is 4% of what amount?
    A. $4000.00   B. $64.00   C. $400.00   D. $6.40   E. NG   35.____

36. $\frac{N}{12} = \frac{13}{39}$
    A. 4   B. 3   C. 13   D. 36   E. NG   36.____

37. -4+2 =
    A. -6   B. -2   C. 2   D. 8   E. NG   37.____

38. 5N = 8N − 12
    N =
    A. 5/8   B. 4   C. 3   D. 13   E. NG   38.____

39. $\dfrac{16}{-8} =$ 39.____

    A. 2   B. 8   C. 12   D. -2   E. NG

40. $2a - 4 = 14 - a$ 40.____
    $a =$
    A. 6   B. 3 1/3   C. 5   D. 10   E. NG

KEY (CORRECT ANSWERS)

1.	C	11.	D	21.	D	31.	C
2.	B	12.	C	22.	D	32.	C
3.	E	13.	A	23.	C	33.	D
4.	C	14.	E	24.	B	34.	D
5.	A	15.	A	25.	D	35.	A
6.	A	16.	D	26.	C	36.	A
7.	B	17.	D	27.	B	37.	B
8.	E	18.	D	28.	C	38.	B
9.	A	19.	B	29.	B	39.	D
10.	B	20.	A	30.	E	40.	A

6 (#1)

SOLUTIONS TO PROBLEMS

1. $17{,}136 \div 34 = 504$

2. $141{,}606 - 94{,}679 = 46{,}927$

3. $8342 \div 86 = 97$

4. $1\frac{2}{3} + 1\frac{5}{6} = 1\frac{4}{6} + 1\frac{5}{6} = 2\frac{9}{6} = 3\frac{1}{2}$

5. $128.94 \div 3 = 42.98$

6. $709 \times 864 = 612{,}576$

7. $138{,}057 - 54{,}368 = 83{,}689$

8. $3\frac{3}{5} \div \frac{9}{10} = \frac{18}{5} \times \frac{10}{9} = \frac{180}{45} = 4$

9. $21.441 \div 7 = 3.063$

10. $\frac{9}{10} - \frac{1}{2} = \frac{9}{10} - \frac{5}{10} = \frac{4}{10} = \frac{2}{5}$

11. $\frac{2}{3} \times 2\frac{1}{4} = \frac{2}{3} \times \frac{9}{4} = \frac{18}{12} = 1\frac{1}{2}$

12. $7646 + 6799 + 3389 + 6597 = 24{,}431$

13. $\frac{5}{6} + 1\frac{3}{4} = \frac{10}{12} + 1\frac{9}{12} = 1\frac{19}{12} = 2\frac{7}{12}$

14. $22.3 - 1.21 = 21.09 = 21.1$ rounded to nearest tenth

15. $9.05 \times 5.9 = 53.395 = 53$ rounded to two digits

16. $608 \times 970 = 589{,}760$

17. $6567 + 8999 + 6877 + 8789 = 3{,}232$

18. $4987 \times 96 = 478{,}752$

19. $3\frac{1}{3} - 1\frac{3}{4} = 3\frac{4}{12} - 1\frac{9}{12} = 2\frac{16}{12} - 1\frac{9}{12} = 1\frac{7}{12}$

20. 4% of $500 = (.04)($500) = $20

7 (#1)

21. $16 \times 10\frac{3}{4} = \frac{16}{1} \times \frac{43}{4} = = \frac{688}{4} = 172$

22. $\frac{16}{K} = 8,, 16 = 8K, K = 2$

23. $4.35 \times .32 = 1.3920 = 1.4$ rounded to nearest tenth

24. $2\frac{1}{2}\%$ of $50 = (.025)(\$50) = \$1.25$

25. $6267.38 \div 89 = 70.42$

26. $\frac{\$10}{\$400} = \frac{1}{40} = 2\frac{1}{2}\%$

27. $31.96 \div 68 = 47$

28. $\frac{4}{6} = \frac{N}{24}$, $6N = 96, N = 16$

29. $6 \div 10 = \frac{6}{10} = \frac{3}{5}$

30. $\frac{3}{10} = \frac{15}{N}$, $3N = 150, N = 50$

31. $\frac{3a}{4} = 6, 3a = 24, a = 8$

32. $\frac{\$40}{\$1600} = \frac{1}{40} = 2\frac{1}{2}\%$

33. $\$25 = 5\%$ of x, $\$25 = .05x$, $x = \frac{\$25}{.05} = \$500$

34. $(-3) \times (6) = -18$

35. $\$160 = 4\%$ of x, $\$160 = .04$, $x = \frac{\$160}{.04} = \$4000$

36. $\frac{N}{12} = \frac{13}{39} = \frac{1}{3}$, $3N=12, N = 4$

37. $-4 + 2 = -2$

38. $4N = 8N - 12, -3N = -12, N = 4$

39. $\frac{16}{-8} = -2$

40. $2a - 4 = 14 - a, 3a - 4 = 14, 3a = 18, a = 6$

TEST 2

DIRECTIONS: Each question or incomplete statement is followed by several suggested answers or completions. Select the one that BEST answers the question or completes the statement. *PRINT THE LETTER OF THE CORRECT ANSWER IN THE SPACE AT THE RIGHT.*

1. 6 is what part of 9?
   A. 1/6   B. 1/3   C. 2/3   D. 1 1/2

2. What is 1.48 rounded to tenths?
   A. 1.4   B. 1.5   C. 1.40   D. 1.50

3. If N times 6 is less than 63, then N may be
   A. 378   B. 69   C. 9   D. 12

4. What is the smallest common denominator for 1/5, 1/2, and 1/3?
   A. 2   B. 3   C. 30   D. 10

5. What does CXC mean?
   A. 210   B. 190   C. 200   D. 201

6. ☐ × 3 = 18.
   Which numbers, if put into the box, would make the sentence TRUE?
   A. 3 × 3   B. 4 + 5   C. 9 – 2   D. 12 + 2

7. Two-thirds of what number is 8?
   A. 12   B. 2 2/3   C. 16   D. 24

8. What is 2.0094 rounded to the nearest hundredth?
   A. 2.009   B. 2.01   C. 2.10   D. 2.010

9. Here are decimal fractions written in four bases. Which would be the LARGEST part of the same pie?
   A. 0.3_{four} B. 0.3_{five} C. 0.3_{six} D. 0.3_{eight}

10. Ten thousand is how many hundreds?
    A. 1   B. 10   C. 1000   D. 100

11. Interest is found by using the formula
    A. lwh   B. prh   C. prt   D. hrw

12. What number is 200% of 25%?
    A. 4
    B. 40
    C. No such number
    D. 50

13. What is the value of N in $\frac{25}{75} = \frac{N}{74}$?

14. What is the product of 3 × (-4)?
    A. +12
    B. 1/12
    C. -12
    D. Can't be multiplied

15. What is the square of (4+2)?
    A. 36
    B. 16
    C. 8
    D. 6

16. 0.26 × 558 is approximately
    A. 140
    B. 2300
    C. 1400
    D. 230

17. $\sqrt{1600}$ is equal to
    A. 4
    B. 40
    C. 400
    D. 4000

18. How many hours pass from 9:45 A.M. to 1:30 P.M.?
    A. $8\frac{1}{4}$
    B. $4\frac{1}{4}$
    C. $4\frac{3}{4}$
    D. $3\frac{3}{4}$

19. Without multiplying, find the difference between 29 × 347 and 28 × 346.
    A. 1
    B. 347
    C. 29
    D. 28

20. What is the dividend if the quotient is 8 and the divisor is 2?
    A. 2
    B. 4
    C. 16
    D. 6

21. 5^3 equals
    A. 15
    B. 25
    C. 625
    D. 125

22. Which fraction is expressed in lowest terms?
    A. $\frac{49}{280}$
    B. $\frac{99}{301}$
    C. $\frac{475}{1320}$
    D. $\frac{998}{1106}$

23. 4 × 253 equals
    A. (4×3)+(4×5)+(44×2)
    B. (4×200)+(4×5)+(4×3)
    C. (4×20)+(4×50)+(4×3)
    D. (4×250)+(4×3)

24. Which number comes next in this set: 1248?
    A. 16
    B. 12
    C. 14
    D. 10

25. Which of these is the BEST estimate of 0.80 ÷0.04?
    A. 0.02
    B. 0.20
    C. 2.0
    D. 20

26. By the distributive property of numbers, we know that 246 × z equals
    A. 2Z+4Z+6Z
    B. 200Z×40Z×6Z
    C. 200Z+40Z+6Z
    D. 6Z+4Z+ZZ

27. If (N+4 times 3 is more than 24, you can be sure that N is
    A. more than 8
    B. less than 3
    C. less than 8
    D. more than 4

28. There are 2 black balls and 3 white balls in a hat.
What are the chances that the first one drawn out will be white?
    A. 1 in 2   B. 3 in 5   C. 2 in 3   D. 1 in 3

28.____

29. If N stands for the same number in each of the following, which will be the smallest?
    A. $N + \frac{1}{2}$ B. $N + \frac{1}{3}$ C. $N + \frac{2}{3}$ D. $N + \frac{1}{4}$

29.____

30. By the commutative property of numbers, we know that
    A. □ + △ = △ + □   B. □ × △ = △ ÷ □
    C. □ × △ = △ + □   D. □ - △ = △ - □

30.____

31. By estimation, choose the example which will have the largest quotient.
    A. $23\overline{)401}$ B. $36\overline{)800}$ C. $23\overline{)400}$ D. $46\overline{)801}$

31.____

32. $16\frac{2}{3}$% of $25 is nearest
    A. 25¢   B. $4.00   C. $2.50   D. 40¢

32.____

33. The volume of a right rectangular prism is found by using the formula
    A. lw   B. hr^2 C. w^2h D. lwh

33.____

34. Which of these is a prime number?
    A. 109   B. 378   C. 126   D. 417

34.____

35. If you know that R + S is less than N, then you know that
    A. R + 1/2 is greater than N   B. R + S is greater than 1/2N
    C. 1/2R + 1/2S is less than 1/2N   D. (1/2R) + S is less than 1/2N

35.____

36. Which would tell you that a number is evenly divisible by 9?

36.____

Questions 37-38.

DIRECTIONS: Questions 37 and 28 are to be answered on the basis of the following sets.

    Set K: Los Angeles, Yosemite, Mt. Whitney
    Set L: Chicago, Denver, Los Angeles, Pittsburgh
    Set M: Mt. McKinley, Pikes Peak, Denver

37. How many elements (different places) are in the union of the three sets, K, L, and M?
    A. 3   B. 8   C. 4   D. 11

37.____

38. Which two sets, if any, are disjoint, that is, have no common members? 38.____
    A. M and L   B. M and K   C. L and K   D. No two sets

39. How many x's are there if counted in a base of eight instead of a base of ten? 39.____
    XXXXXXXXXXXXXXXXXXXXX
    A. 25_{eight} B. 21_{eight} C. 26_{eight} D. 168_{eight}

40. The sum of the digits of a five-place numeral is 24. 40.____
    You know the number is evenly divisible (no remainder) by
    A. 4   B. 3   C. 6   D. 8

KEY (CORRECT ANSWERS)

1.	C	11.	C	21.	D	31.	A
2.	B	12.	D	22.	B	32.	B
3.	C	13.	D	23.	D	33.	D
4.	C	14.	C	24.	A	34.	A
5.	B	15.	A	25.	D	35.	C
6.	D	16.	A	26.	C	36.	C
7.	A	17.	B	27.	D	37.	B
8.	B	18.	D	28.	B	38.	B
9.	A	19.	B	29.	C	39.	A
10.	D	20.	C	30.	A	40.	B

SOLUTIONS TO PROBLEMS

1. $\frac{6}{9} = \frac{2}{3}$

2. 1.48 = 1.5 rounded to nearest tenth

3. 6N < 63, so N < 10.5; so N may be 9

4. The smallest common denominator for 5, 2, and 3 is 30.

5. CXC = 190

6. 12÷2×3 = 18

7. $\frac{2}{3}N = 8$, $N = \frac{8}{1} \times \frac{3}{2} = 12$

8. 2.0094 = 2.01 rounded to nearest hundredth

9. $.3_{four} = 3 \times 4^{-1} = .75_{ten}$; $.3_{five} = 3 \times 5^{-1} = .6_{ten}$; $.3_{six} = 3 \times 6^{-1} = .5_{ten}$; $.3_{eight} = 3 \times 8^{-1} = .375_{ten}$
Thus, $.3_{four}$ is largest.

10. 10,000 ÷ 100 = 100

11. I = prt

12. 200% of 25 = (2)(25) = 50

13. $\frac{25}{75} = \frac{1}{3} = \frac{N}{24}$, 3N = 24, N = 8

14. 3×(-4) = -12

15. $(4+2)^2 = 6^2 = 36$

16. .26 × 558 = 145.08 ≈ 140

17. $\sqrt{1600} = 40$

18. 9:45 A.M. to 1:30 P.M. = $3\frac{3}{4}$ hours

19. 29 × 347 − 28 × 347 = 1 × 347 = 347

20. N ÷ 2 = 8, so N = 16

21. $5^3 = 5 \times 5 \times 5 = 125$

6 (#2)

22. $\frac{99}{301}$ is expressed in lowest terms

23. 4 × 253 = (4×250) + (4×3)

24. 1, 2, 3, 8,..... Each number is double its predecessor. Thus, the fifth number = 16

25. .80 ÷ 04 = 29

26. 246 × Z = 200Z + 40Z + 6Z, using the distributive property

27. (N+4) × 3 > 24, N + 4 > 8, N > 4

28. Probability of drawing a white ball = $\frac{3}{2+3}$ = 3 in 5

29. N ÷ 3 is smallest, provided N > 0

30. $\square + \triangle = \triangle + \square$, by the commutative property

31. 401 ÷ 23 is the largest of the given selections

32. $16\frac{2}{3}$% of $25 = $\frac{1}{6}$ × $25 ≈ $4

33. Volume = lwh

34. 109 is a prime number, since its only divisors are 1 and 109

35. If R + S < N, then, 1/2R + 1/2S < 1/2N

36. A number is divisible by 9 if the sum of its digits is divisible by 9

37. The union of sets K, L, M = {Los Angeles, Yosemite, Mt. Whitney, Chicago, Denver, Pittsburgh, Mt. McKinley, Pikes Peak} which is 8 elements.

38. The sets M and K are disjoint, that is, they have no common elements.

39. 21_{ten} = 25_{eight}

40. If the sum of the digits is 24, the number must be divisible by 3, since is divisible by 3.

TEST 3

DIRECTIONS: Each question or incomplete statement is followed by several suggested answers or completions. Select the one that BEST answers the question or completes the statement. *PRINT THE LETTER OF THE CORRECT ANSWER IN THE SPACE AT THE RIGHT.*

1. What is the volume in cubic inches of the item shown at the right?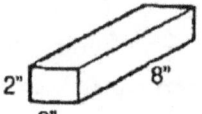
   A. 24
   B. 26
   C. 48
   D. 64
   E. NG

   1.____

2. How much cheaper are a dozen pencils at 49¢ a dozen than a dozen sold at 2 for 9¢?
   A. $4\frac{1}{2}$¢   B. 5¢   C. 54¢   D. 58¢   E. NG

   2.____

Questions 3-5.

DIRECTIONS: Questions 3 through 5 are to be answered on the basis of the following chart.

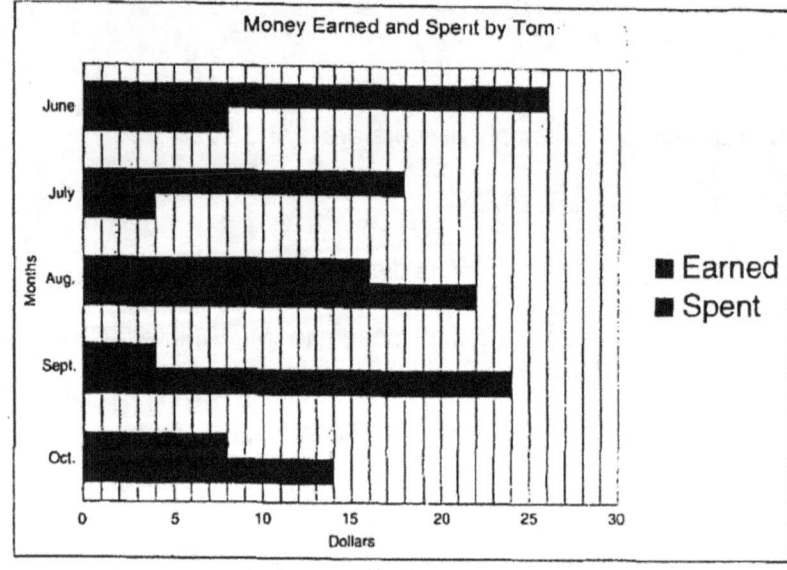

3. In which month(s) did Tom spend over twice as much as he earned?
   A. June and July   B. August   C. September
   D. October   E. None

   3.____

4. How did Tom's earnings compare with what he spent during the 5 months shown?
   A. $1 more   B. He broke even   C. $2 less
   D. $3 more   E. NG

   4.____

2 (#3)

5. In which month did Tom save the MOST money?   5.____
   A. June   B. July   C. August
   D. September   E. October

Questions 6-11.

DIRECTIONS: Several Scouts went by bus to a national park. Questions 6 through 11 are some of their problems.

6. If the bus averages 40 miles per hour for 8 hours, how far will it go in that time?   6.____
   _____ miles.
   A. 5   B. 32   C. 48   D. 320   E. NG

7. At the camp store some candy bars are 3 for 25¢.   7.____
   What would 24 cost at that rate?
   A. $3.00   B. $4.00   C. $6.00   D. $8.00   E. NG

8. We are scheduled to be home at 6:15 P.M.   8.____
   If the trip home takes 1½ hours, when should we start?
   ____ A.M.
   A. 1:45   B. 8:30   C. 9:45   D. 10:45   E. NG

9. At the park, Bill counted 60 trailers. He estimated that this was 1/3 of the total.   9.____
   If so, what was the TOTAL number of trailers?
   A. 180   B. 30   C. 60   D. 20   E. NG

10. Jerry is drawing a map of the park to send home. A 6-inch line will equal 40   10.____
    miles of the park.
    His scale will be
    A. 1 in. = 10 mi.   B. $1\frac{1}{2}$ in. = $6\frac{2}{3}$ C. $1\frac{1}{2}$ in. = 10 mi.
    D. 2 in. = 15 mi.   E. NG

11. How will the Scouts determine equal shares of the cost?   11.____
    A. Total cost × number of people   B. Total cost + the average
    C. Number of people × average   D. Total cost + number of shares

Questions 1-13.

DIRECTIONS: Questions 12 and 13 are to be answered on the basis of the following graph.

DAVID'S DAY (TOTAL 24 HOURS)

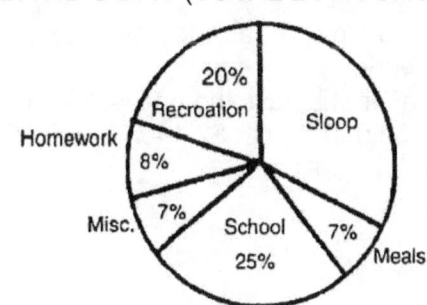

12. What percent of David's day is spent in sleep? 12.____
    A. 33   B. 23   C. 8   D. 37   E. NG

13. How many hours does David spend a day in school? 13.____
    A. 6   B. 7   C. 8   D. 25   E. NG

Questions 14-16.

DIRECTIONS: Questions 14 through 16 are to be answered on the basis of the following chart.

BOXES OF COOKIES SOLD

Ruth	🍪 🍪 🍪 🍪
Betty	🍪 🍪
Nancy	🍪 🍪 🍪 🍪 🍪 🍪
Sue	🍪 🍪 🍪 🍪 🍪
Mary	🍪 🍪 🍪

Each 🍪 equals 5 boxes

14. Who sold 3 times as many boxes as Betty sold? 14.____
    A. Nancy   B. Ruth   C. Mary   D. Sue   E. No one

15. Sue sold how many more boxes than Ruth sold? 15.____
    A. 1   B. 2   C. 6   D. 15   E. NG

16. How many boxes did Betty sell? 16.____
    A. 2   B. 20   C. 11   D. 10   E. NG

Questions 17-19.

DIRECTIONS: Marvin's mother and father both work downtown. Questions 17 through 19 are some of their problems.

17. Marvin's mother and father have one car but are considering buying another for $2,000. Father figures that it will cost $50.00 a month to run each car. 17.____
    How much will it cost to buy the second car and to use it for a year?
    A. $2,050   B. $2,600   C. $2,500   D. $3,200   E. NG

18. The total cost for a babysitter is $7.00 a day for a 5-day week. Mother's take-home pay is $3,740 for 48 weeks' work. 18.____
    How much is left of her yearly pay after she pays the babysitter for 48 weeks?
    A. $1,480   B. $1,680   C. $2,060   D. $2,140   E. NG

19. Father and Mother together earn $12,000 a year.
To find how much Father earns a month, you would
    A. divide sum of both salaries by 2; then divide by 12
    B. subtract Mother's salary from sum of both salaries; multiply by 12
    C. divide 12 by sum of both salaries; then subtract Mother's salary
    D. subtract Mother's salary from sum of both; then divide by 12
    E. do none of the above

19.____

20. What is the circumference of the circle shown in the figure at the right? Use $\pi = \frac{1}{7}$
    A. 11 in.
    B. 21 in.
    C. 22 in.
    D. 154 in.
    E. NG

20.____

Questions 21-23.

DIRECTIONS: Questions 21 through 23 are to be answered on the basis of the following chart.

Number of Problems Worked and Time Spent

Pupil	Time	Problems
Larry	1'15"	25
Meg	45"	15
Joe	40"	10
Sue	1'30"	30
Bill	50"	25

21. What was the average number of problems worked?
    A. 15   B. 21   C. 19   D. 25   E. NG

21.____

22. What was the median length of time spent?
    A. 40"   B. 50"   C. 60"   D. 15"   E. NG

22.____

23. Who is the fastest worker per problem?
    A. Meg   B. Sue   C. Joe   D. Bill   E. NG

23.____

Questions 24-26.

DIRECTIONS: Jack is planting a hedge 30 feet long. Questions 24 through 26 are some of his problems.

24. He can put 30 small plants, costing 15¢ each, 12 inches apart. Or, he can put large plants, costing 40¢ each, 18 inches apart.
How much more will it cost to buy the large plants?
    A. No more   B. $3.50   C. $4.50   D. $8.00   E. NG

24.____

25. Hedge clippers cost $30.00. They can be rented for $1.50 a day. Jack would need them for 4 days each year.
   How many years will it take for the rent to equal the cost?
   A. 4½   B. 5   C. 6   D. 7½   E. NG

26. Jack waters the hedge every day for 15 days, every other day for the next 30 years, and twice a week for the following 16 weeks. Each watering costs about 5¢.
   How many years does it cost to water it during this time?
   A. $3.10   B. $3.05   C. $1.90   D. $4.50   E. NG

27. How long is the diagonal line shown in the figure at the right?
   A. 8½'
   B. 14'
   C. 15'
   D. 17'
   E. NG

28. How tall is a flagpole that makes a shadow of 20 feet when a yardstick makes a shadow of 1 foot 6 inches?
   A. 20 ft.   B. 40 ft.   C. 21 ft. 6 in.
   D. 60 ft.   E. NG

29. The figure shown at the right was once a regular prism, but some of the blocks have been taken away.
   How many are left?
   A. 23
   B. 24
   C. 32
   D. 36
   E. NG

30. A mixture formula reads, *Use ½ oz. per pint of water.*
   A pound will make how many gallons?
   A. 1   B. 2   C. 4   D. 8   E. NG

31. If all of x is part of y, and part of y is all of z, you know that
   A. all of x is z   B. y is all of x and all of z
   C. some of x is z   D. none of z is part of x
   E. x must equal 2 of y

32. How many different triangles are there in the figure shown at the right?
   A. 4
   B. 5
   C. 6
   D. 7
   E. NG

33. The amount of $1.00 at 4% interest compounded annually for 5 years is $1.2167.
    What would be the amount for $50.00 at 4% for 5 years?
    A. $52.00   B. $60.00   C. $60.20   D. $60.84   E. $68.35

34. A house that cost 20,000 is rented for $150 a month. Taxes, depreciation, and other costs amount to $600 for a year.
    What percent does the investment net for the year?
    A. 6   B. 4 ½   C. 5   D. 4   E. NG

35. Jim tossed a coin 7 times. It came up heads twice.
    What are the chances that the next toss will be heads?
    A. 1 in 2   B. 5 in 8   C. 3 in 7   D. 1 in 8   E. NG

KEY (CORRECT ANSWERS)

1.	C	11.	D	21.	B	31.	B
2.	B	12.	A	22.	B	32.	D
3.	C	13.	A	23.	D	33.	D
4.	B	14.	A	24.	B	34.	E
5.	A	15.	E	25.	B	35.	A
6.	D	16.	D	26.	A		
7.	E	17.	B	27.	E		
8.	D	18.	C	28.	B		
9.	A	19.	D	29.	D		
10.	C	20.	C	30.	C		

8 (#3)

SOLUTIONS TO PROBLEMS

1. Volume = (2")(3")(8") = 48 cu. in.

2. Difference in price = (.09)(12/2) - .49 = .05

3. In September, he spent $24 but only earned $4

4. Total earnings = $26 + $18 + $16 + $4 + $8 = $72, whereas total spending = $8 + $4 + $22 + $24 + $14 = $72. He broke even.

5. In June, Tom saved $26 - $8 = $18, which was highest

6. (40)(8) = 320 miles

7. (.25)(24/3) = $2.00

8. 6:15 P.M. – 7 ½ hrs. = 10:45 A.M.

9. $60 \div \frac{1}{3}$ = 180 trailers

10. $\frac{40}{6}$ = 1 in. for $6\frac{2}{3}$ mi. = $1\frac{1}{2}$ in. for 10 mi.

11. Total cost ÷ number of shares = cost per share

12. Sleep = 100% - 20% - 8% - 7% - 25% - 7% = 33%

13. Hours in school = (.25)(24) = 6

14. Nancy sold 30 boxes, which is 3 times as many as Betty sold.

15. Sue sold 25 boxes, which is 5 more than Ruth sold.

16. Betty sold 10 boxes.

17. $2,000 + (12)($50) = $2,600

18. $3740 = ($35)(48) = $2060

19. To find Father's monthly earnings, subtract Mother's salary from the sum of both, then divide by 12.

20. Circumference = $(\pi)(7") \approx (3\frac{1}{7}*7")$ = 22 in.

9 (#3)

21. (25+15+10+30+25)/5 = 105 ÷5 = 21

22. Median = 3rd value from lowest to highest = 50 sec.
(Tines are 40", 45", 50", 1'15", 1'30"))

23. Rates per problem are as follows:
Larry: 75 sec/25 = 3 sec; Meg: 45 sec/15 = 3 sec.
Joe: 40 sec/10 = 4 sec; Sue: 90 sec/30 = 3 sec.
Bill: 50 sec/25 = 2 sec; so Bill is fastest.

24. 30 ÷ 1.5 = 20. Then, (20)(.40) – (30)(.15) = $3.50

25. ($1.50)(4) = $6.00 rental cost per year. Then, $30 ÷ $6 = 5 years.

26. Total cost = (.05)(15) + (.05)(15) + (.05)(32) = $3.10

27. Diagonal = $\sqrt{5^2+12^2}$ = $\sqrt{169}$ = 13 ft.

28. Let x = height of flagpole. $\frac{3}{1\frac{1}{2}} = \frac{x}{20}$, $1\frac{1}{2}x = 60$, x = 40 ft.

29. 1st layer: 15 blocks; 2nd layer: 10 blocks; 3rd layer: 8 blocks; 4th layer: 3 blocks.
Total = 36 blocks

30. 1 lb. ÷ $\frac{1}{2}$ oz = 32, Then, 32 pints = $\frac{32}{8}$ = 4 gallons

31. There are 3 possible diagrams.

32. 1 large triangle, 4 separate smaller triangles, 2 "half" triangles. Total of 7 triangles.
There are ACE, BCD, ABD, ADF, FDE, ACD, ADE.

33. (50)($1.2167) = $60.835 ≈ 60.84.

34. ($150)(12) = $1800. Then, $\frac{\$1800}{\$20,600}$ ≈ 8.7%

35. Regardless of the results of previous tosses, the probability that the next toss is heads = ½ = 1 in 2.

EXAMINATION SECTION
TEST 1

DIRECTIONS: Each question or incomplete statement is followed by several suggested answers or completions. Select the one that BEST answers the question or completes the statement. *PRINT THE LETTER OF THE CORRECT ANSWER IN THE SPACE AT THE RIGHT.*

1. Our number system has a base of
    A. 2   B. 5   C. 10   D. 60

2. To find the average weight of the football team,
    A. add and divide
    B. multiply
    C. add
    D. divide the weight of each player

3. The thermometer used to measure the temperature of a school is called
    A. Centigrade
    B. Fahrenheit
    C. fever thermometer
    D. gauge

4. The value of a fraction is changed when the same number is _____ to both numerator and denominator.
    A. added
    B. divided
    C. multiplied
    D. reduced to both terms of the fraction

5. Stores buy their merchandise from firms called
    A. commissioners
    B. retail firms
    C. factories
    D. wholesale firms

6. The amount of money you borrow is called the
    A. amount
    B. discount
    C. principal
    D. bank discount

7. An angle of 75° is called a(n) _____ angle.
    A. acute   B. obtuse   C. straight   D. right

8. The rate of interest could be found by the formula
    A. I = Prt   B. r = i/pt   C. r = Pt   D. I = P/Rt

9. If three sides of one triangle are equal to the three sides of the other, the triangles are
    A. equilateral
    B. right triangles
    C. scalene
    D. congruent

10. A rectangular solid could be called a(n) 10.____
    A. plane   B. irregular figure
    C. polygon   D. prism

11. A written promise to repay the face of a loan is a 11.____
    A. refund   B. promissory note
    C. dividend   D. deposit

12. The ² written above the s in the formula As² means 12.____
    A. 2s   B. s × s   C. s + s   D. s/2

13. Selling price includes cost plus profit plus 13.____
    A. expenses   B. profit   C. loss   D. net price

14. When numbers are used to express how many or how much of units of measure, they are called 14.____
    A. digits   B. denominate numbers
    C. integers   D. whole numbers

15. The square of a number is that number multiplied by 15.____
    A. two   B. twice the number
    C. four   D. itself

16. When the merchant permits the customer to make a down payment and make regular payments on an article, this form of payment is called 16.____
    A. dues   B. rent
    C. installment buying D. utility payments

17. Circles that have a common center and different radii are _____ circles. 17.____
    A. equal   B. center   C. congruent   D. concentric

18. The United States standard of measure of length is the 18.____
    A. base 10   B. meter
    C. English system   D. metric system

19. If you put money to work for you, the income you receive is called 19.____
    A. income taxes   B. interest
    C. bank discount   D. sales tax

20. A fraction whose numerator is a fraction and denominator is an integer is a _____ fraction. 20.____
    A. common   B. decimal   C. improper   D. complex

KEY (CORRECT ANSWERS)

1.	C	11.	B
2.	A	12.	B
3.	B	13.	A
4.	A	14.	B
5.	D	15.	D
6.	C	16.	C
7.	A	17.	D
8.	B	18.	C
9.	D	19.	B
10.	D	20.	D

SOLUTIONS TO PROBLEMS

1. 10 is the base of our number system. Ex: $456 = (4)(10^2) + (5)(10) + 6$.

2. To find the average weight, add and divide.

3. Fahrenheit degrees would be used for schools.

4. A fraction will change when the same number is added to both numerator and denominator. Ex: Add 5 to both parts of 2/3 to get /8, and 7/8 ≠ 2/3.

5. Stores buy merchandise from wholesale firms.

6. Principal = amount of money borrowed.

7. 75° is an acute angle since it is less than 90°.

8. R = I/(PT) shows rate in terms of interest, principal, and time.

9. If 3 sides of one triangle match 3 sides of a second triangle, they are congruent (SSS).

10. A rectangular solid is a special kind of prism.

11. Promissory note = written promise to repay a loan.

12. $s^2 = s \times s$

13. Selling price includes cost, profit, and expenses.

14. Denominate numbers express units of measure. Ex: 8 gallons.

15. Square of any number = that number times itself. Ex: $4^2 = 4 \times 4 = 16$.

16. Installment buying = down payment + regular payments. Ex: $1000 down payment + $300 payment per month for 2 years.

17. Concentric circles have a common center but different radii. Diagram appears as: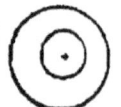

18. The English system is the U.S. standard measure of length. This includes inches, feet, yards, miles, etc.

19. Interest = income received when money is put to work (invested).

20. A complex fraction would contain a fraction within its numerator, denominator, or both.

Ex 1: $\dfrac{\frac{1}{2}}{\frac{1}{3}} = \dfrac{1}{2} \cdot \dfrac{3}{1} = \dfrac{3}{2}$

Ex 2: $\dfrac{1/2}{3} = \dfrac{1}{2} \cdot \dfrac{1}{3} = \dfrac{1}{6}$

Ex 3: $\dfrac{\frac{1}{2}}{3} = \dfrac{1}{1} \cdot \dfrac{3}{2} = \dfrac{3}{2}$

———

TEST 2

DIRECTIONS: Each question or incomplete statement is followed by several suggested answers or completions. Select the one that BEST answers the question or completes the statement. *PRINT THE LETTER OF THE CORRECT ANSWER IN THE SPACE AT THE RIGHT.*

1. Sally is going to Chicago for a visit. The bus fare is $27.85 one way or a round-trip ticket would be $51.56.
   How much can Sally save by buying a round-trip ticket rather than two one-way tickets?
   A. $4.20
   B. $2.07
   C. $4.14
   D. None of the above

   1._____

2. The Webster Junior High School collected $226.45 for Junior Red Cross and $420.55 for the Community Chest. There were 850 students in the school.
   To the NEAREST cent, what was the average contribution?
   A. $.76
   B. $.50
   C. $1.00
   D. None of the above

   2._____

3. Jack borrowed $57.50 from his father and agreed to pay it in twelve monthly payments of $5.00 each.
   How much interest did he pay?
   A. $2.50
   B. $3.50
   C. $7.50
   D. None of the above

   3._____

4. Joe's mother bought a roast weighing 6 ¾ lbs. at 89¢ a pound.
   How much change did she receive from a $10.00 bill?
   A. $3.99
   B. $5.01
   C. $6.01
   D. None of the above

   4._____

5. The Athletic Department paid $45 total tax on 1,000 tickets.
   How much tax was this per ticket?
   A. $.22
   B. $.45
   C. 4.5 cents
   D. None of the above

   5._____

6. Mary bought 4½ yards of lace. She used 1⅔ yards of it on a blouse.
   _____ yards of lace were left.
   A. 3 ⅙
   B. 3 ½
   C. 2 ⅚
   D. None of the above

   6._____

7. The girls are going to make aprons for Junior Red Cross. The pattern calls for ¾ yard of material for one apron.
   They will need _____ yards for 25 aprons.
   A. 33 ⅓
   B. 18 ¾
   C. 20
   D. None of the above

   7._____

2 (#2)

8. Which city on a world map of standard time zones would be NEAR the 75°W? 8.____
   A. Greenwich	B. Sydney
   C. Calcutta	D. None of the above

9. John's father made a down payment on a car and has $1,320 left to pay. 9.____
   He pays $55 each month.
   It will take him _____ months to finish the car payments.
   A. 42	B. 24
   C. 18	D. None of the above

10. Pete bought a board 12 ft. 8 in. long from which he wants to make three shelves. 10.____
    Two of the shelves are 2 ft. 8 in. long, and the third shelf is 1 ft. 6 in. long.
    How long will the piece be that is left over?
    A. 5 ft. 8 in.	B. 5 ft. 10 in.
    C. 6 ft. 10 in.	D. None of the above

11. A factory worker received an increase of 15% in his hourly wages. His former 11.____
    wages were $1.80 per hour.
    How much a week did his wages INCREASE in a forty-hour week?
    A. $21.17	B. $8.00
    C. $10.80	D. None of the above

12. Find the installment price of a washing machine if the down payment is 12.____
    $39.90, the monthly payments are $14.13 for twelve months, and the interest
    charge is $9.86.
    A. $179.52	B. $219.42
    C. $169.56	D. None of the above

13. How many hundreds in 18762? 13.____
    A. 7	B. 87
    C. 187	D. None of the above

14. The football team won 16 games and lost 4 games. 14.____
    What percent of the games played did they win?
    A. 75%	B. 80%
    C. 40%	D. None of the above

15. The bakery boxed doughnuts one half dozen to a box. 15.____
    They will have _____ full boxes if they fry 500 doughnuts.
    A. 41	B. 83
    C. 82	D. None of the above

16. Jane's parents burn fuel oil. They have used 180 gallons. The gauge indicates 16.____
    the tank is 5/8 full.
    The tank holds _____ gallons.
    A. 255	B. 480
    C. 600	D. None of the above

17. _____ tiles, each a 9" square, could be laid in one width of a recreation room that is 25 feet long and 16½ feet wide.
    A. 22
    B. 149
    C. 51
    D. None of the above

17._____

18. The outside diameter of a wheel on Bob's bicycle is 28 inches. The outside diameter of a wheel on his little brother's bicycle is 21 inches. After traveling a mile, the little brother's wheel will make _____ revolutions more.
    A. 1080
    B. 269.5
    C. 240
    D. None of the above

18._____

19. Bill gets 17 ¾ miles per gallon.
    At this rate, he should get _____ miles if he buys 5.6 gallons of gasoline.
    A. 317
    B. 99.4
    C. 85
    D. None of the above

19._____

20. The scale drawing of a house is 1 in. = 12 ft.
    If a room is 33 feet long, a _____ inch line should be used on the blueprint to represent that distance.
    A. 2 ¾
    B. 3.3
    C. 2.1
    D. None of the above

20._____

21. A 2-inch gear makes 75 revolutions per minute.
    A 3-inch fear makes _____ rpm at the same rate of speed.
    A. 12 ½
    B. 112 ½
    C. 50
    D. None of the above

21._____

22. What is the selling price of a radio that cost the dealer $36 and the margin is 40% of the selling price?
    A. $60
    B. $45
    C. $50.40
    None of the above

22._____

23. Mr. Jacks used 35 kwh.
    If the charge is 8¢ a kwh for the first 20 kwh and 5¢ for the remainder, what was the TOTAL charge?
    A. $2.35
    B. $3.35
    C. $4.55
    D. None of the above

23._____

24. Druggists use a unit of measurement of weight called the grain. There are *approximately* 437.5 grains in one ounce.
    There are APPROXIMATELY _____ grains in a pound.
    A. 7000
    B. 5252
    C. 73,400
    D. None of the above

24._____

25. A gasoline tank is 16 ft. high and has a diameter of 14 ft.
    The tank will hold _____ cubic feet of gasoline (use 22/7 for pi) to the NEAREST 10 cu. ft.
    A. 704
    B. 784
    C. 2460
    D. None of the above

25._____

KEY (CORRECT ANSWERS)

1. C
2. A
3. A
4. A
5. C

6. C
7. B
8. D
9. B
10. B

11. C
12. B
13. C
14. B
15. B

16. B
17. A
18. C
19. B
20. A

21. C
22. A
23. A
24. A
25. C

SOLUTIONS TO PROBLEMS

1. Savings = ($27.85)(2) - $51.56 = $4.14

2. Average contribution = ($226.45 + $420.55) ÷ 850 = $647 ÷ 850 ≈ $.76

3. Interest = (12)($5.00) - $57.50 = $2.50

4. $10.00 – (6.75)(.89) = $3.99 change

5. $45 ÷ 1000 = .045 = 4.5 cents tax per ticket

6. 4 1/2 – 1 2/3 = 4 3/6 – 1 4/6 – 1 = 2 5.6 yds, left

7. (3/4)(25) = 18 3/4 yds. needed

8. Refer to world map. None is correct.

9. $1320 ÷ 55 = 24 months

10. 12'8" – 2'8" – 2'8" – 1'6" = 152" – 32" – 32" – 18" = 70" = 5'10"

11. Increase = ($1.80)(.15)(40) = $10.80 per week

12. $39.90 + ($14.13)(12) + $9.96 = $219.42 installment price

13. 18,762 ÷ 100 = 187 with remainder of 62. So, there are 187 hundreds in 18,762.

14. Percent won = 16/20 = 80%

15. 500 ÷ 6 = 83 1/3, which means 83 full boxes + 1/3 of a box

16. 180 gallons represents 3/8 of the entire tank. Thus, the tank's capacity = 180 ÷ 3/8 = 480 gallons

17. 25' = 300" and 16 1/2' = 198". Now, 300 ÷ 9 = 33 1.3 and 198 ÷ 9 = 22. Then the number of tiles that could fit in 1 width = 22. (The actual number of tiles that could fit in the entire room = (22)(33) = 726)

18. 1 revolution of Bob's bicycle = $2\pi = (2 \times \frac{22}{7} \times 14) = 88"$

    1 revolution of his brother's bicycle = $2\pi = (2 \times \frac{22}{7} \times 10.5) = 66"$

19. $(17\frac{3}{4})(5.6) = (17.75)(5.6) = 99.4$ miles

20. 33 ÷ 12 = 2 3/4-inch line needed.

21. Let x = rpm. 2/3 = x/75. Solving, x = 50.
    Note: Size of gear is inversely related to rpm.

22. Let x = selling price. Then, $36 = .60x. Solving, x = $60.

23. Total charge = (.08)(20) + (.05)(15) = $2.35

24. (437.5)(16) = 7000 grains in a pound (approx.)

25. Volume = $(\pi)(7^2)(16) \approx 2460$ cu. ft.

ARITHMETICAL REASONING
EXAMINATION SECTION
TEST 1

DIRECTIONS: Each question or incomplete statement is followed by several suggested answers or completions. Select the one that BEST answers the question or completes the statement. *PRINT THE LETTER OF THE CORRECT ANSWER IN THE SPACE AT THE RIGHT.*

1. The initial mark-up in a store is 40%; mark-downs are 5%; shortages 1%; cash discounts 5%; alteration costs 5%; expenses 25%.
   The maintained mark-up is
   A. 34% B. 39% C. 36.4% D. 30%

   1.____

2. A buyer of TV sets wishes to maintain a mark-up of 37½% after all mark-downs are taken. Of 25 sets costing $150 each, he sells 20 at $265.
   How much can he mark-down the remaining 5 sets and still realize his mark-up objective?
   A. $166 B. $150 C. $140 D. $125

   2.____

3. An article originally selling for $12 and costing $8 was marked down to $10. Assuming the same mark-up, what is the present market value of its cost?
   A. $6.68 B. $8.00 C. $5.67 D. $6.86

   3.____

4. What is the *on* percentage of trade discounts of 20% and 10%?
   A. 70 B. 85 C. 72 D. 80

   4.____

5. Canadian cost of a sweater is $40. Packing and labor cost $5.00; ad valorem duty, 40%; specific duty, 65¢; rate of exchange, .9091.
   What is the duty in American currency?
   A. $16.96 B. $16.36 C. $18.00 D. $18.60

   5.____

6. A bolt of cloth measures 40 yards. The following yardages are sold: 4½, 5¾, 6⅞.
   How many yards are left?
   A. 23⅞ B. 22½ C. 22⅞ D. 24⅜

   6.____

7. A shirt manufacturer has 76½ yards of broadcloth to be used for shirts. If each shirt takes 2½ yards, how many shirts can he make?
   A. 38 B. 30 C. 19 D. 31

   7.____

8. Subtract 1.003 from 24.5.
   A. 24.003 B. 12.42 C. 23.2 D. 23.497

   8.____

9. A store carries a stock amounting to $265,830.25. Cash discounts, on the average, amount to 5¼%.
   How much are the cash discounts?
   A. $13,956.09   B. $1,395.61   C. $139.56   D. $1.39

   9._____

10. If the sales in a department totaled $67,507.50 and the average sale was $22.50, how many transactions were there?
    A. 3,000   B. 300   C. 30,000   D. 0

    10._____

11. A department store reports a decrease in sales of 5.5% for this year.
    If this year's sales are $275,825,000, last year's sales were
    A. $291,878,000   B. $290,995,000
    C. $260,655,000   D. $290,788,000

    11._____

12. For the current year, the sales volume in a store was $50,000,000. Other income amounted to $1,500,000, operating expenses were $10,000,000; cost of goods sold, $37,500,000.
    What is the percent of net profit based on retail?
    A. 10   B. 8   C. 50   D. 13

    12._____

13. If this year's sales shown an increase of 300% over last year, this year's sales are how many times last year's sales?
    A. 3   B. 1¹/₃   C. 4   D. ¼

    13._____

14. Net sales in a shop amounted to $374,000; returns were 10%; allowances 5%.
    What were the gross sales?
    A. $430,100   B. $415,000   C. $411,400   D. $440,000

    14._____

15. If the average sale in a store is expected to rise 5% over last year, and the number of transactions increases 3%, what percentage of increase in dollar sales volume should be planned?
    A. 8   B. 4   C. 8.15   D. 8.51

    15._____

16. The billed cost on an invoice is $300; freight charges, $10; cash discount, 2%; the retail value of the merchandise is $525.
    The mark-up percent on retail is
    A. 40.9   B. 42   C. 69   D. 69.5

    16._____

17. A hat costing $30.00 is to be given a mark-up of 45% on retail.
    The retail should be
    A. $43.50   B. $46.40   C. $55.40   D. $54.50

    17._____

18. Retail price $40 per unit; mark-up 40% of retail; transportation charge, $1 per unit.
    Find billed cost that store can pay.
    A. 23   B. $24   C. $23.75   D. $24.75

    18._____

19. A buyer plans to spend $17,000 at retail for merchandise at a mark-up of 34%.
He finds a special value at $3,000 that he can sell for $6,000.
What mark-up percentage does he need on the balance of his purchases in order to achieve his planned 34%?
  A. 35   B. 19.9   C. 15   D. 22.5

19.____

20. A store has a gross margin of 40% and reductions of 13%. Cash discount on purchases are not credited to the department. There are no alteration costs.
What is the initial mark-up?
  A. 46%   B. 53%   C. 27%   D. 26%

20.____

21. A dress is to retail for $35 with a mark-up of 40% of retail.
The cost of the dress to the retailer was
  A. $25   B. $21   C. $14   D. $20

21.____

22. The cost is $1.20 and the desired gross profit is 40% of retail.
The retail price should be
  A. $1.60   B. $1.68   C. $2.00   D. $2.40

22.____

23. The realized mark-up on a TV set is $50. The mark-up is 25% of retail.
The cost of the TV set to the retailer was
  A. $200   B. $125   C. $100   D. $150

23.____

24. Farnum, a salesman, earns $19.20 per hour for 40 hours a week, with time and a half for all hours over 40 per week. Last week, his total earnings were $940.80.
How many hours did he work last week?
  A. 46   B. 49   C. 47   D. 48

24.____

25. Dane & Clarke, partners, share profits in a 5:3 ratio. Dane's share of the profit for this year was $12,000 more than Clarke's share.
Clarke's share of the net profit was
  A. $30,000   B. $48,000   C. $36,000   D. $18,000

25.____

KEY (CORRECT ANSWERS)

1.	C	11.	A
2.	D	12.	B
3.	A	13.	C
4.	C	14.	D
5.	A	15.	C
6.	C	16.	A
7.	B	17.	D
8.	D	18.	A
9.	A	19.	B
10.	A	20.	A

21.	B
22.	C
23.	D
24.	A
25.	D

SOLUTIONS TO PROBLEMS

1. $5 + 5 - 1 = 9\%$. Then, $(40\%)(91) = 36.4\%$.

2. $(25)(\$150) = \$3{,}750$, and $\$3{,}750 \div .625 = \$6000$ total selling price of all sets. $\$6{,}000 - (20)(\$265) = \$700$; $700 \div 5 = \$140$ selling price for each of the last 5 sets. Markdown amount = $\$265 - \$140 = \$125$.

3. When the article's original selling price was $12, its cost was $8.00. If the article's original selling price were to be $10, it would cost $(8.00)/12.00×10.00) = $6.67.

4. Resulting percentage = $(1.20)(1-.10) = .72 = 72\%$.

5. $(\$45)(.40) = \$18 + .65 = \$18.65$. Then, $(\$18.65)(.9091) = \$16.95$, closest to $16.96 in American currency.

6. $40 - 4½ - 5¾ - 6^7/_8 = 22^7/_8$ yds.

7. $76½ \div 2½ = 30.6$, rounded down to 30 shirts.

8. $24.5 - 1.003 = 23.497$.

9. $(\$265{,}830)(.0525) = \$13{,}956.09$.

10. $\$67{,}507.50 \div \$22.50 = 3{,}000$ transactions.

11. $\$275{,}825{,}000 \div .945 = \$291{,}878{,}000$.

12. $\$50{,}000{,}000 + \$1{,}500{,}000 - \$10{,}000{,}000 = \$37{,}500{,}000 = \$4{,}000{,}000$. Then, $\$4{,}000{,}000 \div \$50{,}000{,}000 = .08 = 8\%$.

13. An increase of 300% over x = 4x, so sales are 4 times as large.

14. Gross sales = $374,000 ÷ .85 = $440,000.

15. $(1.05)(1.03) = 1.0815$, which represents an 8.15% increase in dollar sales volume.

16. $525 - $310 = $215; then, $215/$525 = 40.9%.

17. $30 will represent 55% of retail amount. Thus, retail will be $30 ÷ .55 = $54.50.

18. $(\$40)(.60) - \$1 = \$23$.

19. $(\$17{,}000)(1.34) = \$22{,}780$. Then, $\$22{,}780 - \$6000 = \$16{,}780$. Also, $\$17{,}000 - \$3{,}000 = \$14{,}000$. Finally, $(\$16{,}780 - \$14{,}000) \div \$14{,}000 \approx 19.9\%$.

20. Let x = markup percent. Then, x – 40/x = .13. Solving, x = 46.

21. Cost = ($35)(.60) = $21.

22. Let x = retail price. Then, $1.20 = .60x. Solving, x = $2.00.

23. $50 = 25% of retail, so retail = $200. Thus, cost = $200 - $50 = $150.

24. Let x = overtime hours. Then, ($19.20)(40) + $28.80x = $940.80. Solving, x = 6 total.

25. 5x = 3x - $12,000. So, x = $6,000. Clarke's share = (3)($6,000) = $18,000.

TEST 2

DIRECTIONS: Each question or incomplete statement is followed by several suggested answers or completions. Select the one that BEST answers the question or completes the statement. *PRINT THE LETTER OF THE CORRECT ANSWER IN THE SPACE AT THE RIGHT.*

1. Assume that you require 77 dozen felt practice golf balls.
   Which of the following represents the LOWEST bid for these balls?
   A. 41¢ per half-dozen less a 3% discount
   B. 83¢ per dozen less a 7½% discount
   C. 85¢ per dozen less a 10% discount
   D. $65.00 less a series discount of 3%, 2%

   1.____

2. Assume that you require 1,944 rulers, packed 12 to the box, 18 boxes to the carton.
   Which of the following represents the LOWEST bid for these rulers?
   A. 5½ ¢ per ruler
   B. 6¢ for the first 750 rulers; 5½¢ for the next 750 rulers; 4½¢ for every ruler thereafter
   C. $11.85 per carton
   D. $110 less series discounts of 2%, 1%.

   2.____

3. Assume that you require 20 cartons of colored raffia, cellophane wrapped in one lb. packages, 50 packages to the carton.
   Which of the following represents the LOWEST bid for the raffia?
   A. 8¢ per lb.; 15¢ per carton packaging charge; 20¢ per carton delivery charge
   B. 9¢ per lb. less a 3% discount
   C. 10¢ per lb. for the first 150 lbs.; 9¢ per lb. for the next 200 lbs.; 80 for each lb. thereafter
   D. $83.50 less a 4½% discount

   3.____

4. Assume that you require 50 yards of table felt, 48" wide, and 12 yards of table felt, 72" wide.
   Which of the following represents the LOWEST bid for this felt?
   A. 32¢ per yard (48" wide), 40¢ per yard (72" wide)
   B. 34¢ per yard (48" wide), 43¢ per yard (72" wide); series discounts of 5%, 3%
   C. 360 per yard (48" wide), 41¢ per yard (72" wide); 8% discount, packing charge 75¢
   D. $23.00 for the order, 9% discount, packing charge 50¢

   4.____

5. If the cost of 3 erasers is 5¢, the cost of 2½ dozen erasers is
   A. 18¢　　　　B. 37½¢　　　　C. 50¢　　　　D. 31½¢

   5.____

6. A circle graph of a budget shows the expenditure of 26.2% for housing, 28.4% for food, 12% for clothing, 12.7% for taxes, and the balance for miscellaneous items.
   The percent for miscellaneous items is
   A. 31.5   B. 79.3   C. 20.7   D. 68.5

7. The cost of a broadloom rug measuring 4 feet by 6 feet, at $6.30 per square yard, is
   A. $16.80   B. $50.40   C. $37.60   D. $21.00

8. The number of tiles each measuring 2 inches by 3 inches needed for a wall 3 feet high and 5 feet long is
   A. 180   B. 30   C. 360   D. 60

9. Assume that you require 4 tons of fertilizer. The fertilizer is packed in 100 pound bags.
   Which of the following represents the LOWEST bid for the fertilizer?
   A. 6¢ per pound
   B. $5.50 per bag
   C. $7.00 for each of the first 30 bags; $5.00 for each bag thereafter
   D. $500.00 less 3½% discount

10. Assume pencils are packed 5 gross to the case. A buyer requires 3,800 pencils each for three departments and 2,700 pencils for another department. Assume that the vendor will ship unbroken cases only directly to each department.
    How many cases should he buy?
    A. 21   B. 22   C. 48   D. 49

11. Assume that a buyer had to purchase 40,000 lbs. of salt.
    Which one of the following bids should he accept, assuming quality, service, and delivery terms are all the same?
    A. 1¢ per pound, 2%-30 days   B. 99¢ per 100 lbs., 1%-30 days
    C. $19 per ton, 1%-30 days   D. $18 per ton, net-30 days

12. Which one of the following four bids represent the BEST value, assuming delivery costs amount to $100?
    A. $1,000 f.o.b. buyer, less 2%-10 days
    B. $900 f.o.b. seller, less 2%-10 days
    C. $975 delivered, net cash 30 days
    D. $990 f.o.b. buyer, less 1%-10 days

13. Suppose that four suppliers make the following offers to sell 2,000 units of a particular commodity.
    Which one is the MOST advantageous proposal?
    A. $10 list, less 40% and 5%
    B. $5 cost, plus 20% to cover overhead and profit
    C. $10 list, less 20% and 20%
    D. $5 cost, plus 10% overhead and 10% for profit

14. Suppose that you purchase 100 units of an item at a list of $1 per unit less 40% and 10%, and less 2% if paid within 10 days.
    If payment is made within the 10-day limit, the amount of the payment should be
    A. $52.92   B. $54.00   C. $58.80   D. $60.00

15. Assume that the 2018 cost of living factor was 100 and that a certain product was selling that year for $5 per unit. Assume further that at the present time the cost of living factor is 150.
    If the selling price of the product increased 10% more than the cost of living during this period, at the present time the product would be selling for _____ per unit.
    A. $8.25   B. $10.50   C. $16.50   D. $7.75

16. A certain food is sold in 4 ounce cans at 10 for $1.00 and in 1 pound cans at 3 for $1.00.
    The savings in price per ounce by purchasing the food in the larger can is _____ cents/ounce.
    A. .53   B. .35   C. .42   D. .68

17. After an article is discounted at 25%, it sells for $375.
    The ORIGINAL price of the article was
    A. $93.75   B. $350   C. $35   D $500

18. Assume that you require 1,440 pencils, packed 12 to the box, 24 boxes to the carton.
    Which of the following represents the LOWEST bid for these pencils?
    A. 2¢ per pencil   B. $6.50 per carton
    C. 27¢ per box less a 4% discount   D. $40 less a 3% discount

19. If erasers cost 8¢ each for the first 250, 7¢ each for the next 250, and 5¢ for every eraser thereafter, how many erasers may be purchased for $50?
    A. 600   B. 750   C. 850   D. 1,000

20. Assume that a buyer saves $14 on the purchase of an item that is discounted at 25%
    The amount of money that the buyer must pay for the item is
    A. $42   B. $52   C. $54   D. $56

Questions 21-24.

DIRECTIONS: Questions 21 through 24 are to be answered on the basis of the following method of obtaining a reorder point: multiply the monthly rate of consumption by the lead time (in months) and add the minimum balance.

21. If the lead time is one-half month, the minimum balance is 6 units, and the monthly rate of consumption is 4 units, then the reorder point is _____ units.
    A. 4   B. 6   C. 8   D. 12

22. If the reorder point is 25 units, the lead time is 3 months, and the minimum balance is 10 units, then the average monthly rate of consumption is _____ units.
    A. 3   B. 5   C. 6   D. 10

23. If the reorder point is 400 units, the lead time is 2 months, and the monthly rate of consumption is 150 units, then the minimum balance is _____ units.
    A. 50   B. 100   C. 150   D. 200

24. If the reorder point is 75 units, the monthly rate of consumption is 60 units, and the minimum balance is 45 units, then the lead time is _____ month(s).
    A. ½   B. 1   C. 2   D. 4

25. A purchasing office has 4,992 special requisitions to be processed. Working alone, Buyer A could process these in 30 days; working alone, Buyer B could process these in 40 days; working alone, Buyer C could process these in 60 days.
    The LEAST number of days in which Buyers A, B, and C working together can process these 4,992 special requisitions is APPROXIMATELY _____ days.
    A. 14   B. 20   C. 34   D. 45

KEY (CORRECT ANSWERS)

1.	C		11.	D
2.	B		12.	C
3.	D		13.	A
4.	B		14.	A
5.	C		15.	A
6.	C		16.	C
7.	A		17.	D
8.	C		18.	A
9.	B		19.	B
10.	B		20.	A

21. C
22. B
23. B
24. A
25. A

SOLUTIONS TO PROBLEMS

1. Bid A = (.82)(77)(.97) ≈ $61.25
   Bid B = (.83)(77)(.925) ≈ $59.12
   Bid C = (.85)(77)(.90) ≈ $58.91
   Bid D = ($65.00)(.97)(.98) ≈ $61.79.
   Thus, Bid C is lowest.

2. Bid A = (.055)(1944) = $106.92
   Bid B = (.06)(750) + (.055)(750) + (.045)(444) = $106.23
   Bid C = ($11.85)(9) = $106.65
   Bid D = ($110)(.98)(.99) ≈ $106.72.
   Thus, Bid B is lowest.

3. Bid A = (.08)(1000) + (.15)(20) + (.20)(20) = $87.00
   Bid B = (.09)(1000) = $87.30
   Bid C = (.10)(150) + (.09)(200) + (.08)(650) = $85.00
   Bid D = ($83.50)(.955) ≈ $79.74
   Thus, Bid D is lowest.

4. Bid A = (.32)(50) + (.40)(12) = $20.80
   Bid B = (.34)(50) + (.43)(12) = $22.16; so ($22.16)(.95)(.97) ≈ $20.42
   Bid C = (.36)(50) + (.41)(12) = $22.92; so ($22.92)(.92) + .75 ≈ $21.84
   Bid D = ($23.00)(.91) + .50 = $21.43
   Bid B is lowest.

5. (2½)(12) = 30 erasers, which will cost (.05)(10) = 50¢

6. 100 − 26.2 − 28.4 − 12 − 12.7 = 20.7% for miscellaneous items.

7. 24 ÷ 9 = $2^{2}/_{3}$ sq. yds. Then, ($6.30)($2^{2}/_{3}$) = $16.80

8. 3'2" = 18; 5'3" = 20. Thus, (18)(20) = 360 tiles.

9. Bid A = (.06)(8000) = $480
   Bid B = ($5.50)(80) = $440
   Bid C = ($7.00)(30) + ($5.00)(50) = $460
   Bid D = ($500)(.965) = $482.59
   Thus, Bid B is lowest.

10. 5 gross = 5(144); 3800 will be 6 unbroken cases × 3 = 18.
    2700 will be 4 unbroken cases = 4
    ―――
    22

11. Bid A = (.01)(40,000)(.98) = $392.00
    Bid B = (.99)(400)(.99) = $392.04
    Bid C = ($19)(20)(.99) = $376.20
    Bid D = ($18)(20) = $360.00
    Bid D is lowest.

12. A. 1,000 – 2% = 980
    B. 900 + 100 – 2% = 980
    C. 975
    D. 990 – 9.90 = 980.10
    C is best value.

13. Proposal A: ($10)(.60)(.95) = $5.70
    Proposal B: $5 + ($5)(.20) = $6.00
    Proposal C: ($10)(.80)(.80) = $6.40
    Proposal D: $5 + (.20)($5) = $6.00
    Proposal A is lowest.

14. Payment = ($100)(.60)(.90)(.98) = $52.92

15. Present cost = ($5)(1.50)(1.10) = $8.25

16. 40 ounces for $1.00 in smaller cans means 2.5 cents per ounce. For the larger cans, (3)(16) = 48 ounces for $1.00, which means 2.083 cents per ounce. The savings is approximately .42 cents per ounce.

17. Original price = $375 ÷ 75 = $500

18. Bid A = (1440)(.02) = $28.80
    Bid B = (1440 ÷ 288)($6.50) = $32.50
    Bid C = [(144 ÷ 12)(.27)][.96] = $31.10
    Bid D = ($40)(.97) = $38.80
    Bid A is lowest.

19. 250 erasers cost (250)(.08) = $20
    500 erasers cost $20 + (250)(.07) = $37.50
    The number of additional erasers = ($50 - $37.50) ÷ .05 = 250
    Total number of erasers = 750

20. $14 ÷ .25 = $56. Then, $56 - $14 = $42

21. (4)(.5) + 6 = 8 units

22. Let x = monthly rate. Then, (x)(3) + 10 = 25. Solving, x = 5 units.

23. Let x = minimum balance. (150)(2) + x = 400. Solving, x = 100 units.

24. Let x = lead time. (60)(x) + 45 = 75. Solving, x = ½ month.

25. Buyer A does 4992 ÷ 30 ≈ 166 per day.
    Buyer B does 4992 ÷ 40 ≈ 125 per day.
    Buyer C does 4992 ÷ 60 ≈ 83 per day.
    Working together, approximately 374 requisitions are done per day.
    Finally, 4992 ÷ 374 ≈ 13, closest to 14 in selections.

CLERICAL ABILITIES TEST
EXAMINATION SECTION
TEST 1

DIRECTIONS: Each question or incomplete statement is followed by several suggested answers or completions. Select the one that BEST answers the question or completes the statement. *PRINT THE LETTER OF THE CORRECT ANSWER IN THE SPACE AT THE RIGHT.*

Questions 1-10.

DIRECTIONS: Questions 1 through 10 consist of lines of names, dates, and numbers. For each question, you are to choose the option (A, B, C, or D) in Column II which EXACTLY matches the information in Column I. *PRINT THE LETTER OF THE CORRECT ANSWER IN THE SPACE AT THE RIGHT.*

SAMPLE QUESTION

Column I
Schneider 11/16/75 581932

Column II
A. Schneider 11/16/75 518932
B. Schneider 11/16/75 581932
C. Schnieder 11/16/75 581932
D. Shnieder   11/16/75 518932

The correct answer is B. Only Option B shows the name, date, and number exactly as they are in Column I. Option A has a mistake in the number. Option C has a mistake in the name. Option D has a mistake in the name and in the number. Now answer Questions 1 through 10 in the same manner.

Column I
1. Johnston 12/26/74 659251

Column II
A. Johnson   12/23/74 659251
B. Johston   12/26/74 659251
C. Johnston 12/26/74 695251
D. Johnston 12/26/74 659251

1.____

2. Allison 1/26/75 9939256

A. Allison   1/26/75 9939256
B. Alisson   1/26/75 9939256
C. Allison   1/26/76 9399256
D. Allison   1/26/75 9993356

2.____

3. Farrell 2/12/75 361251

A. Farell   2/21/75 361251
B. Farrell   2/12/75 361251
C. Farrell   2/21/75 361251
D. Farrell   2/12/75 361151

3.____

4. Guerrero 4/28/72 105689
   A. Guererro 4/28/72 105689
   B. Guerrero 4/28/72 105986
   C. Guerrero 4/28/72 105869
   D. Guerrero 4/28/72 105689

4.____

5. McDonnell 6/05/73 478215
   A. McDonnell 6/15/73 478215
   B. McDonnell 6/05/73 478215
   C. McDonnell 6/05/73 472815
   D. MacDonell 6/05/73 478215

5.____

6. Shepard 3/31/71 075421
   A. Sheperd 3/31/71 075421
   B. Shepard 3/13/71 075421
   C. Shepard 3/31/71 075421
   D. Shepard 3/13/71 075241

6.____

7. Russell 4/01/69 031429
   A. Russell 4/01/69 031429
   B. Russell 4/10/69 034129
   C. Russell 4/10/69 031429
   D. Russell 4/01/69 034129

7.____

8. Phillips 10/16/68 961042
   A. Philipps 10/16/68 961042
   B. Phillips 10/16/68 960142
   C. Phillips 10/16/68 961042
   D. Philipps 10/16/68 916042

8.____

9. Campbell 11/21/72 624856
   A. Campbell 11/21/72 624856
   B. Campbell 11/21/72 624586
   C. Campbell 11/21/72 624686
   D. Campbel 11/21/72 624856

9.____

10. Patterson 9/18/71 76199176
    A. Patterson 9/18/72 76191976
    B. Patterson 9/18/71 76199176
    C. Patterson 9/18/72 76199176
    D. Patterson 9/18/71 76919176

10.____

Questions 11-15.

DIRECTIONS: Questions 11 through 15 consist of groups of numbers and letters which you are to compare. For each question, you are to choose the option (A, B, C, or D) in Column I which EXACTLY matches the group of numbers and letters given in Column I.

SAMPLE QUESTION

Column I
B92466

Column II
A. B92644
B. B94266
C. A92466
D. B92466

The correct answer is D. Only Option D in Column II shows the group of numbers and letters EXACTLY as it appears in Column I. Now answer Questions 11 through 15 in the same manner.

	Column I		Column II	
11.	925AC5	A. 952CA5 B. 925AC5 C. 952AC5 D. 925CA6		11.____
12.	Y006925	A. Y060925 B. Y006295 C. Y006529 D. Y006925		12.____
13.	J236956	A. J236956 B. J326965 C. J239656 D. J932656		13.____
14.	AB6952	A. AB6952 B. AB9625 C. AB9652 D. AB6925		14.____
15.	X259361	A. X529361 B. X259631 C. X523961 D. X259361		15.____

Questions 16-25.

DIRECTIONS: Each of questions 16 through 25 consists of three lines of code letters and three lines of numbers. The numbers on each line should correspond with the code letters on the same line in accordance with the table below.

Code Letter	S	V	W	A	Q	M	X	E	G	K
Corresponding Number	0	1	2	3	4	5	5	7	8	9

On some of the lines, an error exists in the coding. Compare the letters and numbers in each question carefully. If you find an error or errors on:
  only one of the lines in the question, mark your answer A;
  any two lines in the question, mark your answer B;
  all three lines in the question, mark your answer C;
  none of the lines in the question, mark your answer D.

SAMPLE QUESTION

WQGKSXG	2489068
XEKVQMA	6591453
KMAESXV	9527061

In the above sample, the first line is correct since each code letter listed has the correct corresponding number. On the second line, an error exists because code letter E should have the number 7 instead of the number 5. On the third line, an error exists because the code letter A should have the number 3 instead of the number 2. Since there are errors in two of the three lines, the correct answer is B. Now answer Questions 16 through 25 in the same manner.

16. SWQEKGA   0247983   16.____
     KEAVSXM   9731065
     SSAXGKQ   0036894

17. QAMKMVS   4259510   17.____
     MGGEASX   5897306
     KSWMKWS   9125920

18. WKXQWVE   2964217   18.____
     QKXXQVA   4966413
     AWMXGVS   3253810

19. GMMKASE   8559307   19.____
     AWVSKSW   3210902
     QAVSVGK   4310189

20. XGKQSMK   6894049   20.____
     QSVKEAS   4019730
     GSMXKMV   8057951

21. AEKMWSG   3195208   21.____
     MKQSVQK   5940149
     XGQAEVW   6843712

22. XGMKAVS   6858310   22.____
     SKMAWEQ   0953174
     GVMEQSA   8167403

23. VQSKAVE   1489317   23.____
     WQGKAEM   2489375
     MEGKAWQ   5689324

24. XMQVSKG   6541098   24.____
     QMEKEWS   4579720
     KMEVGKG   9571983

25. GKVAMEW   88912572   25.____
    AXMVKAE   3651937
    KWAGMAV   9238531

Questions 26-35.

DIRECTIONS: Each of Questions 26 through 35 consists of a column of figures. For each question, add the column of figures and choose the correct answer from the four choices given.

26.   5,665.43   26.____
      2,356.69
      6,447.24
      7,239.65

   A. 20,698.01   B. 21,709.01
   C. 21,718.01   D. 22,609.01

27.   817,209.55   27.____
      264,354.29
       82,368.76
      849,964.89

   A. 1,893.977.49   B. 1,989,988.39
   C. 2,009,077.39   D. 2,013,897.49

28.   156,366.89   28.____
      249,973.23
      823,229.49
       56,869.45

   A. 1,286,439.06   B. 1,287,521.06
   C. 1,297,539.06   D. 1,296,421.06

29.   23,422.15   29.____
      149,696.24
      238,377.53
       86,289.79
      505,533.63

   A. 989,229.34   B. 999,879.34
   C. 1,003,330.34   D. 1,023,329.34

6 (#1)

30.   2,468,926.70
     656,842.28
      49,723.15
     832,369.59

   A. 3,218,062.72   B. 3,808,092.72
   C. 4,007,861.72   D. 4,818,192.72

30.____

31.   524,201.52
    7,775,678.51
    8,345,299.63
  40,628,898.08
  31,374,670.07

   A. 88,646,647.81   B. 88,646,747.91
   C. 88,648,647.91   D. 88,648,747.81

31.____

32.   6,824,829.40
     682,482.94
  5,542,015.27
     775,678.51
  7,732,507.25

   A. 21,557,513.37   B. 21,567,513.37
   C. 22,567,503.37   D. 22,567,513.37

32.____

33.   22,109,405.58
    6,097,093.43
    5,050,073.99
    8,118,050.05
    4,313,980.82

   A. 45,688,593.87   B. 45,688,603.87
   C. 45,689,593.87   D. 45,689,603.87

33.____

34.   79,324,114.19
  99,848,129.74
  43,331,653.31
  41,610,207.14

   A. 264,114,104.38   B. 264,114,114.38
   C. 265,114,114.38   D. 265,214,104.38

34.____

35. 33,729,653.94
     5,959,342.58
    26,052,715.47
     4,452,669.52
     7,079,953.59

    A. 76,374,334.10   B. 76,375,334.10
    C. 77,274,335.10   D. 77,275,335.10

Questions 36-40.

DIRECTIONS: Each of Questions 36 through 40 consists of a single number in Column I and four options in Column II. For each question, you are to choose the option (A, B, C, or D) in Column II which EXACTLY matches the number in Column I.

SAMPLE QUESTION

Column I   Column II
5965121   A. 5956121
                  B. 5965121
                  C. 5966121
                  D. 5965211

The correct answer is B. Only Option B shows the number EXACTLY as it appears in Column I. Now answer Questions 36 through 40 in the same manner.

Column I   Column II
36. 9643242   A. 9643242
                      B. 9462342
                      C. 9642442
                      D. 9463242

37. 3572477   A. 3752477
                      B. 3725477
                      C. 3572477
                      D. 3574277

38. 5276101   A. 5267101
                      B. 5726011
                      C. 5271601
                      D. 5276101

39. 4469329   A. 4496329
                      B. 4469329
                      C. 4496239
                      D. 4469239

8 (#1)

40. 2326308   A. 2236308
             B. 2233608
             C. 2326308
             D. 2323608

40.____

KEY (CORRECT ANSWERS)

1.	D	11.	B	21.	A	31.	D
2.	A	12.	D	22.	C	32.	A
3.	B	13.	A	23.	B	33.	B
4.	D	14.	A	24.	D	34.	A
5.	B	15.	D	25.	A	35.	C
6.	C	16.	D	26.	B	36.	A
7.	A	17.	C	27.	D	37.	C
8.	C	18.	A	28.	A	38.	D
9.	A	19.	D	29.	C	39.	B
10.	B	20.	B	30.	C	40.	C

TEST 2

DIRECTIONS: Each question or incomplete statement is followed by several suggested answers or completions. Select the one that BEST answers the question or completes the statement. *PRINT THE LETTER OF THE CORRECT ANSWER IN THE SPACE AT THE RIGHT.*

Questions 1-5.

DIRECTIONS: Each of Questions 1 through 5 consists of a name and a dollar amount. In each question, the name and dollar amount in Column II should be an EXACT copy of the name and dollar amount in Column I. If there is:
  a mistake only in the name, mark your answer A;
  a mistake only in the dollar amount, mark your answer B;
  a mistake in both the name and the dollar amount, mark your answer C;
  no mistake in either the name or the dollar amount, mark your answer D.

SAMPLE QUESTION

Column I
George Peterson
$125.50

Column II
George Petersson
$125.50

Compare the name and dollar amount in Column II with the name and dollar amount in Column I. The name *Petersson* in Column II is spelled *Peterson* in Column I. The amount is the same in both columns. Since there is a mistake only in the name, the answer to the sample question is A. Now answer Questions 1 through 5 in the same manner.

	Column I	Column II	
1.	Susanne Shultz $3440	Susanne Schultz $3440	1.____
2.	Anibal P. Contrucci $2121.61	Anibel P. Contrucci $2112.61	2.____
3.	Eugenio Mendoza $12.45	Eugenio Mendozza $12.45	3.____
4.	Maurice Gluckstadt $4297	Maurice Gluckstadt $4297	4.____
5.	John Pampellonne $4656.94	John Pammpellonne $4566.94	5.____

Questions 6-11.

DIRECTIONS: Each of Questions 6 through 11 consist of a set of names and addresses, which you are to compare. In each question, the name and addresses in Column II should be an EXACT copy of the name and address in Column I. If there is:
- a mistake only in the name, mark your answer A;
- a mistake only in the address, mark your answer B;
- a mistake in both the name and address, mark your answer C;
- no mistake in either the name or address, mark your answer D.

SAMPLE QUESTION

Column I
Michael Filbert
456 Reade Street
New York, N.Y. 10013

Column II
Michael Filbert
645 Reade Street
New York, N.Y. 10013

Since there is a mistake only in the address (the street number should be 456 instead of 645), the answer to the sample question is B. Now answer Questions 6 through 11 in the same manner.

	Column I	Column II	
6.	Hilda Goettelmann 55 Lenox Rd. Brooklyn, N.Y. 11226	Hilda Goettelman 55 Lenox Ave. Brooklyn, N.Y. 11226	6.____
7.	Arthur Sherman 2522 Batchelder St. Brooklyn, N.Y. 11235	Arthur Sharman 2522 Batcheder St. Brooklyn, N.Y. 11253	7.____
8.	Ralph Barnett 300 West 28 Street New York, New York 10001	Ralph Barnett 300 West 28 Street New York, New York 10001	8.____
9.	George Goodwin 135 Palmer Avenue Staten Island, New York 10302	George Godwin 135 Palmer Avenue Staten Island, New York 10302	9.____
10.	Alonso Ramirez 232 West 79 Street New York, N.Y. 10024	Alonso Ramirez 223 West 79 Street New York, N.Y. 10024	10.____
11.	Cynthia Graham 149-34 83 Street Howard Beach, N.Y. 11414	Cynthia Graham 149-35 83 Street Howard Beach, N.Y. 11414	11.____

Questions 12-20.

DIRECTIONS: Questions 12 through 20 are problems in subtraction. For each question do the subtraction and select your answer from the four choices given.

12. 232,921.85
    -179,587.68

    A. 52,433.17   B. 52,434.17
    C. 53,334.17   D. 53,343,17

    12.____

13. 5,531,876.29
    -3,897,158.36

    A. 1,634,717.93   B. 1,644,718.93
    C. 1,734,717.93   D. 1,7234,718.93

    13.____

14. 1,482,658.22
    -937,925.76

    A. 544,633.46   B. 544,732.46
    C. 545,632.46   D. 545,732.46

    14.____

15. 937,828.17
    -259,673.88

    A. 678,154.29   B. 679,154.29
    C. 688,155.39   D. 699,155.39

    15.____

16. 760,412.38
    -263,465.95

    A. 496,046.43   B. 496,946.43
    C. 496,956.43   D. 497,046.43

    16.____

17. 3,203,902.26
    -2,933,087.96

    A. 260,814.30   B. 269,824.30
    C. 270,814.30   D. 270,824.30

    17.____

18. 1,023,468.71
    -934,678.88

    A. 88,780.83   B. 88,789.83
    C. 88,880.83   D. 88,889.83

    18.____

4 (#2)

19. 831,549.47
    -772,814.78

    A. 58,734.69 B. 58,834.69
    C. 59,735.69 D. 59,834.69

19._____

20. 6,306,181.74
    -3,617,376.99

    A. 2,687,904.99 B. 2,688,904.99
    C. 2,689,804.99 D. 2,799,905.99

20._____

Questions 21-30.

DIRECTIONS: Each of Questions 21 through 30 consists of three lines of code letters and three lines of numbers. The numbers on each line should correspond with the code letters on the same line in accordance with the table below.

Code Letter	J	U	B	T	Y	D	K	R	L	P
Corresponding Number	0	1	2	3	4	5	6	7	8	9

On some of the lines, an error exists in the coding. Compare the letters and numbers in each question carefully. If you find an error or errors on:
  only *one* of the lines in the question, mark your answer A;
  any *two* lines in the question, mark your answer B;
  all *three* lines in the question, mark your answer C;
  none of the lines in the question, mark your answer D.

SAMPLE QUESTION

  BJRPYUR   2079417
  DTBPYKJ   5328460
  YKLDBLT   4685283

In the above sample, the first line is correct since each code letter listed has the correct corresponding number. On the second line, an error exists because code letter P should have the number 9 instead of the number 8. The third line is correct since each code letter listed has the correct corresponding number. Since there is an error in *one* of the three lines, the correct answer is A. Now answer Questions 21 through 30 in the same manner.

21. BYPDTJL   2495308
     PLRDTJU   9815301
     DTJRYLK   5207486

21._____

22. RPBYRJK   7934706
     PKTYLBU   9624821
     KDLPJYR   6489047

22._____

84

5 (#2)

23.	TPYBUJR	3942107		23.____
	BYRKPTU	2476931		
	DUKPYDL	5169458		
24.	KBYDLPL	6345898		24.____
	BLRKBRU	2876261		
	JTULDYB	0318542		
25.	LDPYDKR	8594567		25.____
	BDKDRJL	2565708		
	BDRPLUJ	2679810		
26.	PLRLBPU	9858291		26.____
	LPYKRDJ	88936750		
	TDKPDTR	3569527		
27.	RKURPBY	7617924		27.____
	RYUKPTJ	7426930		
	RTKPTJD	7369305		
28.	DYKPBJT	5469203		28.____
	KLPJBTL	6890238		
	TKPLBJP	3698209		
29.	BTPRJYL	2397148		29.____
	LDKUTYR	8561347		
	YDBLRPJ	4528190		
30.	ULPBKYT	1892643		30.____
	KPDTRBJ	6953720		
	YLKJPTB	4860932		

6 (#2)

KEY (CORRECT ANSWERS)

1.	A	11.	D	21.	B
2.	C	12.	C	22.	C
3.	A	13.	A	23.	D
4.	D	14.	B	24.	B
5.	C	15.	A	25.	A
6.	C	16.	B	26.	C
7.	C	17.	C	27.	A
8.	D	18.	B	28.	D
9.	A	19.	A	29.	B
10.	B	20.	B	30.	D

RECORD KEEPING
EXAMINATION SECTION
TEST 1

DIRECTIONS: Each question or incomplete statement is followed by several suggested answers or completions. Select the one that BEST answers the question or completes the statement. *PRINT THE LETTER OF THE CORRECT ANSWER IN THE SPACE AT THE RIGHT.*

Questions 1-7.

DIRECTIONS: In answering Questions 1 through 7, use the following master list. For each question, determine where the name would fit on the master list. Each answer choice indicates right before or after the name in the answer choice.

    Aaron, Jane
    Armstead, Brendan
    Bailey, Charles
    Dent, Ricardo
    Grant, Mark
    Mars, Justin
    Methieu, Justine
    Parker, Cathy
    Sampson, Suzy
    Thomas, Heather

1. Schmidt, William
   A. Right before Cathy Parker
   B. Right after Heather Thomas
   C. Right after Suzy Sampson
   D. Right before Ricardo Dent

2. Asanti, Kendall
   A. Right before Jane Aaron
   B. Right after Charles Bailey
   C. Right before Justine Methieu
   D. Right after Brendan Armstead

3. O'Brien, Daniel
   A. Right after Justine Methieu
   B. Right before Jane Aaron
   C. Right after Mark Grant
   D. Right before Suzy Sampson

4. Marrow, Alison
   A. Right before Cathy Parker
   B. Right before Justin Mars
   C. Right before Mark Grant
   D. Right after Heather Thomas

5. Grantt, Marissa
   A. Right before Mark Grant
   B. Right after Mark Grant
   C. Right after Justin Mars
   D. Right before Suzy Sampson

1.____
2.____
3.____
4.____
5.____

6. Thompson, Heath   6._____
   A. Right after Justin Mars   B. Right before Suzy Sampson
   C. Right after Heather Thomas   D. Right before Cathy Parker

DIRECTIONS: Before answering Question 7, add in all of the names from Questions 1 through 6. Then fit the name in alphabetical order based on the new list.

7. Francisco, Mildred   7._____
   A. Right before Mark Grant   B. Right after Marissa Grantt
   C. Right before Alison Marrow   D. Right after Kendall Asanti

Questions 8-10.

DIRECTIONS: In answering Questions 8 through 10, compare each pair of names and addresses. Indicate whether they are the same or different in any way.

8. William H. Pratt, J.D.   William H. Pratt, J.D.   8._____
   Attourney at Law   Attorney at Law
   A. No differences   B. 1 difference
   C. 2 differences   D. 3 differences

9. 1303 Theater Drive,; Apt. 3-B   1330 Theatre Drive,; Apt. 3-B   9._____
   A. No differences   B. 1 difference
   C. 2 differences   D. 3 differences

10. Petersdorff, Briana and Mary   Petersdorff, Briana and Mary   10._____
    A. No differences   B. 1 difference
    C. 2 differences   D. 3 differences

11. Which of the following words, if any, are misspelled?   11._____
    A. Affordable   B. Circumstansial
    C. Legalese   D. None of the above

Questions 12-13.

DIRECTIONS: Questions 12 and 13 are to be answered on the basis of the following table.

Standardized Test Results for High School Students in District #1230

	English	Math	Science	Reading
High School 1	21	22	15	18
High School 2	12	16	13	15
High School 3	16	18	21	17
High School 4	19	14	15	16

The scores for each high school in the district were averaged out and listed for each subject tested. Scores of 0-10 are significantly below College Readiness Standards. 11-15 are below College Readiness, 16-20 meet College Readiness, and 21-25 are above College Readiness.

12. If the high schools need to meet or exceed in at least half the categories in order to NOT be considered "at risk," which schools are considered "at risk"?
    A. High School 2
    B. High School 3
    C. High School 4
    D. Both A and C

13. What percentage of subjects did the district as a whole meet or exceed College Readiness standards?
    A. 25%
    B. 50%
    C. 75%
    D. 100%

Questions 14-15.

DIRECTIONS: Questions 14 and 15 are to be answered on the basis of the following information.

You have seven employees working as a part of your team: Austin, Emily, Jeremy, Christina, Martin, Harriet, and Steve. You have just sent an e-mail informing them that there will be a mandatory training session next week. To ensure that work still gets done, you are offering the training twice during the week: once on Tuesday and also on Thursday. This way half the employees will still be working while the other half attend the training. The only other issue is that Jeremy doesn't work on Tuesdays and Harriet doesn't work on Thursdays due to compressed work schedules.

14. Which of the following is a possible attendance roster for the first training session?
    A. Emily, Jeremy, Steve
    B. Steve, Christina, Harriet
    C. Harriet, Jeremy, Austin
    D. Steve, Martin, Jeremy

15. If Harriet, Christina, and Steve attend the training session on Tuesday, which of the following is a possible roster for Thursday's training session?
    A. Jeremy, Emily, and Austin
    B. Emily, Martin, and Harriet
    C. Austin, Christina, and Emily
    D. Jeremy, Emily, and Steve

Questions 16-20.

DIRECTIONS: In answering Questions 16 through 20, you will be given a word and will need to choose the answer choice that is MOST similar or different to the word.

16. Which word means the SAME as *annual*?
    A. Monthly
    B. Usually
    C. Yearly
    D. Constantly

17. Which word means the SAME as *effort*?
    A. Energy
    B. Equate
    C. Cherish
    D. Commence

18. Which word means the OPPOSITE of *forlorn*?
    A. Neglected
    B. Lethargy
    C. Optimistic
    D. Astonished

19. Which word means the SAME as *risk*?
    A. Admire
    B. Hazard
    C. Limit
    D. Hesitant

4 (#1)

20. Which word means the OPPOSITE of *translucent*? 20.____
   A. Opaque   B. Transparent   C. Luminous   D. Introverted

21. Last year, Jamie's annual salary was $50,000. Her boss called her today 21.____
   to inform her that she would receive a 20% raise for the upcoming year. How
   much more money will Jamie receive next year?
   A. $60,000   B. $10,000   C. $1,000   D. $51,000

22. You and a co-worker work for a temp hiring agency as part of their office 22.____
   staff. You both are given 6 days off per month. How many days off are you
   and your co-worker given in a year?
   A. 24   B. 72   C. 144   D. 48

23. If Margot makes $34,000 per year and she works 40 hours per week for 23.____
   all 52 weeks, what is her hourly rate?
   A. $16.34/hour   B. $17.00/hour   C. $15.54/hour   D. $13.23/hour

24. How many dimes are there in $175.00? 24.____
   A. 175   B. 1,750   C. 3,500   D. 17,500

25. If Janey is three times as old as Emily, and Emily is 3, how old is Janey? 25.____
   A. 6   B. 9   C. 12   D. 15

KEY (CORRECT ANSWERS)

1.	C		11.	B
2.	D		12.	A
3.	A		13.	D
4.	B		14.	B
5.	B		15.	A
6.	C		16.	C
7.	A		17.	A
8.	B		18.	C
9.	C		19.	B
10.	A		20.	A

21. B
22. C
23. A
24. B
25. B

TEST 2

DIRECTIONS: Each question or incomplete statement is followed by several suggested answers or completions. Select the one that BEST answers the question or completes the statement. *PRINT THE LETTER OF THE CORRECT ANSWER IN THE SPACE AT THE RIGHT.*

Questions 1-6.

DIRECTIONS: Questions 1 through 6 are to be answered on the basis of the following information.

item	name of item to be ordered
quantity	minimum number that can be ordered
beginning amount	amount in stock at start of month
amount received	amount receiving during month
ending amount	amount in stock at end of month
amount used	amount used during month
amount to order	will need at least as much of each item as used in the previous month
unit price	cost of each unit of an item
total price	total price for the order

Item	Quantity	Beginning	Received	Ending	Amount Used	Amount to Order	Unit Price	Total Price
Pens	10	22	10	8	24	20	$0.11	$2.20
Spiral notebooks	8	30	13	12			$0.25	
Binder clips	2 boxes	3 boxes	1 box	1 box			$1.79	
Sticky notes	3 packs	12 packs	4 packs	2 packs			$1.29	
Dry erase markers	1 pack (dozen)	34 markers	8 markers	40 markers			$16.49	
Ink cartridges (printer)	1 cartridge	3 cartridges	1 cartridge	2 cartridges			$79.99	
Folders	10 folders	25 folders	15 folders	10 folders			$1.08	

1. How many packs of sticky notes were used during the month? 1.____
   A. 16   B. 10   C. 12   D. 14

2. How many folders need to be ordered for next month? 2.____
   A. 15   B. 20   C. 30   D. 40

3. What is the total price of notebooks that you will need to order? 3.____
   A. $6.00   B. $0.25   C. $4.50   D. $2.75

4. Which of the following will you spend the second most money on? 4.____
   A. Ink cartridges   B. Dry erase markers
   C. Sticky notes   D. Binder clips

5. How many packs of dry erase markers should you order? 5.____
   A. 1   B. 8   C. 12   D. 0

91

6. What will be the total price of the file folders you order? 6._____
   A. $20.16   B. $21.60   C. $10.80   D. $4.32

Questions 7-11.

DIRECTIONS: Questions 7 through 11 are to be answered on the basis of the following table.

Number of Car Accidents, By Location and Cause, for 2014						
	Location 1		Location 2		Location 3	
Cause	Number	Percent	Number	Percent	Number	Percent
Severe Weather	10		25		30	
Excessive Speeding	20	40	5		10	
Impaired Driving	15		15	25	8	
Miscellaneous	5		15		2	4
TOTALS	50	100	60	100	50	100

7. Which of the following is the third highest cause of accidents for all three locations? 7._____
   A. Severe Weather
   B. Impaired Driving
   C. Miscellaneous
   D. Excessive Speeding

8. The average number of Severe Weather accidents per week at Location 3 for the year (52 weeks) was MOST NEARLY 8._____
   A. 0.57   B. 30   C. 1   D. 1.25

9. Which location had the LARGEST percentage of accidents caused by Impaired Driving? 9._____
   A. 1   B. 2   C. 3   D. Both A and B

10. If one-third of the accidents at all three locations resulted in at least one fatality, what is the LEAST amount of deaths caused by accidents last year? 10._____
    A. 60   B. 106   C. 66   D. 53

11. What is the percentage of accidents caused by miscellaneous means from all three locations in 2014? 11._____
    A. 5%   B. 10%   C. 13%   D. 25%

12. How many pairs of the following groups of letters are exactly alike? 12._____
    ACDOBJ   ACDBOJ
    HEWBWR   HEWRWB
    DEERVS   DEERVS
    BRFQSX   BRFQSX
    WEYRVB   WEYRVB
    SPQRZA   SQRPZA

    A. 2   B. 3   C. 4   D. 5

Questions 13-19.

DIRECTIONS: Questions 13 through 19 are to be answered on the basis of the following information.

In 2012, the most current information on the American population was finished. The information was compiled by 200 volunteers in each of the 50 states. The territory of Puerto Rico, a sovereign of the United States, had 25 people assigned to compile data. In February of 2010, volunteers in each state and sovereign began collecting information. In Puerto Rico, data collection finished by January 31st, 2011, while work in the United States was completed on June 30, 2012. Each volunteer gathered data on the population of their state or sovereign. When the information was compiled, volunteers sent reports to the nation's capital, Washington, D.C. Each volunteer worked 20 hours per month and put together 10 reports per month. After the data was compiled in total, 50 people reviewed the data and worked from January 2012 to December 2012.

13. How many reports were generated from February 2010 to April 2010 in Illinois and Ohio?
    A. 3,000 B. 6,000 C. 12,000 D. 15,000

14. How many volunteers in total collected population data in January 2012?
    A. 10,000 B. 2,000 C. 225 D. 200

15. How many reports were put together in May 2012?
    A. 2,000 B. 50,000 C. 100,000 D. 100,250

16. How many hours did the Puerto Rican volunteers work in the fall (September-November)?
    A. 60 B. 500 C. 1,500 D. 0

17. How many workers were compiling or reviewing data in July 2012?
    A. 25 B. 50 C. 200 D. 250

18. What was the total amount of hours worked by Nevada volunteers in July 2010?
    A. 500 B. 4,000 C. 4,500 D. 5,000

19. How many reviewers worked in January 2013?
    A. 75 B. 50 C. 0 D. 25

20. John has to file 10 documents per shelf. How many documents would it take for John to fill 40 shelves?
    A. 40 B. 400 C. 4,500 D. 5,000

21. Jill wants to travel from New York City to Los Angeles by bike, which is approximately 2,772 miles. How many miles per day would Jill need to average if she wanted to complete the trip in 4 weeks?
    A. 100 B. 89 C. 99 D. 94

22. If there are 24 CPU's and only 7 monitors, how many more monitors do you need to have the same amount of monitors as CPU's?
    A. Not enough information
    B. 17
    C. 31
    D. 0

23. If Gerry works 5 days a week and 8 hours each day, and John works 3 days a week and 10 hours each day, how many more hours per year will Gerry work than John?
    A. They work the same amount of hours.
    B. 450
    C. 520
    D. 832

24. Jimmy gets transferred to a new office. The new office has 25 employees, but only 16 are there due to a blizzard. How many coworkers was Jimmy able to meet on his first day?
    A. 16   B. 25   C. 9   D. 7

25. If you do a fundraiser for charities in your area and raise $500 total, how much would you give to each charity if you were donating equal amounts to 3 of them?
    A. $250.00   B. $167.77   C. $50.00   D. $111.11

KEY (CORRECT ANSWERS)

1.	D	11.	C
2.	B	12.	B
3.	A	13.	C
4.	C	14.	A
5.	D	15.	C
6.	B	16.	C
7.	D	17.	B
8.	A	18.	B
9.	A	19.	C
10.	D	20.	B

21. C
22. B
23. C
24. A
25. B

TEST 3

DIRECTIONS: Each question or incomplete statement is followed by several suggested answers or completions. Select the one that BEST answers the question or completes the statement. *PRINT THE LETTER OF THE CORRECT ANSWER IN THE SPACE AT THE RIGHT.*

Questions 1-3.

DIRECTIONS: In answering Questions 1 through 3, choose the correctly spelled word.

1. A. allusion   B. alusion   C. allusien   D. allution   1.____

2. A. altitude   B. alltitude   C. atlitude   D. altlitude   2.____

3. A. althogh   B. allthough   C. althrough   D. although   3.____

Questions 4-9.

DIRECTIONS: In answering Questions 4 through 9, choose the answer that BEST completes the analogy.

4. Odometer is to mileage as compass is to   4.____
    A. speed   B. needle   C. hiking   D. direction

5. Marathon is to race as hibernation is to   5.____
    A. winter   B. dream   C. sleep   D. bear

6. Cup is to coffee as bowl is to   6.____
    A. dish   B. spoon   C. food   D. soup

7. Flow is to river as stagnant is to   7.____
    A. pool   B. rain   C. stream   D. canal

8. Paw is to cat as hoof is to   8.____
    A. lamb   B. horse   C. lion   D. elephant

9. Architect is to building as sculptor is to   9.____
    A. museum   B. chisel   C. stone   D. statue

Questions 10-14.

DIRECTIONS: Questions 10 through 14 are to be answered on the basis of the following graph.

Population of Carroll City Broken Down by Age and Gender (in Thousands)			
Age	Female	Male	Total
Under 15	60	60	120
15-23		22	
24-33		20	44
34-43	13	18	31
44-53	20		67
64 and Over	65	65	130
TOTAL	230	232	462

10. How many people in the city are between the ages of 15-23?
    A. 70   B. 46,000   C. 70,000   D. 225,000

11. Approximately what percentage of the total population of the city was female aged 24-33?
    A. 10%   B. 5%   C. 15%   D. 25%

12. If 33% of the males have a job and 55% of females don't have a job, which of the following statements is TRUE?
    A. Males have approximately 2,600 more jobs than females.
    B. Females have approximately 49,000 more jobs than males.
    C. Females have approximately 26,000 more jobs than males.
    D. None of the above statements are true.

13. How many females between the ages of 15-23 live in Carroll City?
    A. 67,000   B. 24,000   C. 48,000   D. 91,000

14. Assume all males 44-53 living in Carroll City are employed. If two-thirds of males age 44-53 work jobs outside of Carroll City, how many work within city limits?
    A. 31,333
    B. 15,667
    C. 47,000
    D. Cannot answer the question with the information provided

Questions 15-16.

DIRECTIONS: Questions 15 and 16 are labeled as shown. Alphabetize them for filing. Choose the answer that correctly shows the order.

15. (1) AED
    (2) OOS
    (3) FOA
    (4) DOM
    (5) COB

   A. 2-5-4-3-2   B. 1-4-5-2-3   C. 1-5-4-2-3   D. 1-5-4-3-2

16. Alphabetize the names of the people. Last names are given last.
    (1) Lindsey Jamestown
    (2) Jane Alberta
    (3) Ally Jamestown
    (4) Allison Johnston
    (5) Lyle Moreno

   A. 2-1-3-4-5   B. 3-4-2-1-5   C. 2-3-1-4-5   D. 4-3-2-1-5

17. Which of the following words is misspelled?
    A. disgust
    B. whisper
    C. locale
    D. none of the above

Questions 18-21.

DIRECTIONS: Questions 18 through 21 are to be answered on the basis of the following list of employees.

   Robertson, Aaron
   Bacon, Gina
   Jerimiah, Trace
   Gillette, Stanley
   Jacks, Sharon

18. Which employee name would come in third in alphabetized list?
    A. Robertson, Aaron
    B. Jerimiah, Trace
    C. Gillette, Stanley
    D. Jacks, Sharon

19. Which employee's first name starts with the letter in the alphabet that is five letters after the first letter of their last name?
    A. Jerimiah, Trace
    B. Bacon, Gina
    C. Jacks, Sharon
    D. Gillette, Stanley

20. How many employees have last names that are exactly five letters long?
    A. 1   B. 2   C. 3   D. 4

21. How many of the employees have either a first or last name that starts with the letter "G"?
   A. 1   B. 2   C. 4   D. 5

Questions 22-25.

DIRECTIONS: Questions 22 through 25 are to be answered on the basis of the following chart.

Bicycle Sales (Model #34JA32)							
Country	May	June	July	August	September	October	Total
Germany	34	47	45	54	56	60	296
Britain	40	44	36	47	47	46	260
Ireland	37	32	32	32	34	33	200
Portugal	14	14	14	16	17	14	89
Italy	29	29	28	31	29	31	177
Belgium	22	24	24	26	25	23	144
Total	176	198	179	206	208	207	1166

22. What percentage of the overall total was sold to the German importer?
   A. 25.3%   B. 22%   C. 24.1%   D. 23%

23. What percentage of the overall total was sold in September?
   A. 24.1%   B. 25.6%   C. 17.9%   D. 24.6%

24. What is the average number of units per month imported into Belgium over the first four months shown?
   A. 26   B. 20   C. 24   D. 31

25. If you look at the three smallest importers, what is their total import percentage?
   A. 35.1%   B. 37.1%   C. 40%   D. 28%

KEY (CORRECT ANSWERS)

1.	A		11.	B
2.	A		12.	C
3.	D		13.	C
4.	D		14.	B
5.	C		15.	D
6.	D		16.	C
7.	A		17.	D
8.	B		18.	D
9.	D		19.	B
10.	C		20.	B

21. B
22. A
23. C
24. C
25. A

TEST 4

DIRECTIONS: Each question or incomplete statement is followed by several suggested answers or completions. Select the one that BEST answers the question or completes the statement. *PRINT THE LETTER OF THE CORRECT ANSWER IN THE SPACE AT THE RIGHT.*

Questions 1-6.

DIRECTIONS: In answering Questions 1 through 6, choose the sentence that represents the BEST example of English grammar.

1.
   A. Joey and me want to go on a vacation next week.
   B. Gary told Jim he would need to take some time off.
   C. If turning six years old, Jim's uncle would teach Spanish to him.
   D. Fax a copy of your resume to Ms. Perez and me.

   1._____

2.
   A. Jerry stood in line for almost two hours.
   B. The reaction to my engagement was less exciting than I thought it would be.
   C. Carlos and me have done great work on this project.
   D. Two parts of the speech needs to be revised before tomorrow.

   2._____

3.
   A. Arriving home, the alarm was tripped.
   B. Jonny is regarded as a stand up guy, a responsible parent, and he doesn't give up until a task is finished.
   C. Each employee must submit a drug test each month.
   D. One of the documents was incinerated in the explosion.

   3._____

4.
   A. As soon as my parents get home, I told them I finished all of my chores.
   B. I asked my teacher to send me my missing work, check my absences, and how did I do on my test.
   C. Matt attempted to keep it concealed from Jenny and me.
   D. If Mary or him cannot get work done on time, I will have to split them up.

   4._____

5.
   A. Driving to work, the traffic report warned him of an accident on Highway 47.
   B. Jimmy has performed well this season.
   C. Since finishing her degree, several job offers have been given to Cam.
   D. Our boss is creating unstable conditions for we employees.

   5._____

6.
   A. The thief was described as a tall man with a wiry mustache weighing approximately 150 pounds.
   B. She gave Patrick and I some more time to finish our work.
   C. One of the books that he ordered was damaged in shipping.
   D. While talking on the rotary phone, the car Jim was driving skidded off the road.

   6._____

Questions 7-9.

DIRECTIONS: Questions 7 through 9 are to be answered on the basis of the following graph.

Ice Lake Frozen Flight (2002-2013)		
Year	Number of Participants	Temperature (Fahrenheit)
2002	22	4°
2003	50	33°
2004	69	18°
2005	104	22°
2006	108	24°
2007	288	33°
2008	173	9°
2009	598	39°
2010	698	26°
2011	696	30°
2012	777	28°
2013	578	32°

7. Which two year span had the LARGEST difference between temperatures?
   A. 2002 and 2003
   B. 2011 and 2012
   C. 2008 and 2009
   D. 2003 and 2004

8. How many total people participated in the years after the temperature reached at least 29°?
   A. 2,295   B. 1,717   C. 2,210   D. 4,543

9. In 2007, the event saw 288 participants, while in 2008 that number dropped to 173. Which of the following reasons BEST explains the drop in participants?
   A. The event had not been going on that long and people didn't know about it.
   B. The lake water wasn't cold enough to have people jump in.
   C. The temperature was too cold for many people who would have normally participated.
   D. None of the above reasons explain the drop in participants.

10. In the following list of numbers, how many times does 4 come just after 2 when 2 comes just after an odd number?
    2365247653898632488572486392424
    A. 2   B. 3   C. 4   D. 5

11. Which choice below lists the letter that is as far after B as S is after N in the alphabet?
    A. G   B. H   C. I   D. J

Questions 12-15.

DIRECTIONS: Questions 12 through 15 are to be answered on the basis of the following directory and list of changes.

Directory		
Name	Emp. Type	Position
Julie Taylor	Warehouse	Packer
James King	Office	Administrative Assistant
John Williams	Office	Salesperson
Ray Moore	Warehouse	Maintenance
Kathleen Byrne	Warehouse	Supervisor
Amy Jones	Office	Salesperson
Paul Jonas	Office	Salesperson
Lisa Wong	Warehouse	Loader
Eugene Lee	Office	Accountant
Bruce Lavine	Office	Manager
Adam Gates	Warehouse	Packer
Will Suter	Warehouse	Packer
Gary Lorper	Office	Accountant
Jon Adams	Office	Salesperson
Susannah Harper	Office	Salesperson

Directory Updates:
- Employee e-mail addresses will adhere to the following guidelines: lastnamefirstname@apexindustries.com (ex. Susannah Harper is harpersusannah@apexindustries.com). Currently, employees in the warehouse share one e-mail, distribution@apexindustries.com.
- The "Loader" position will now be referred to as "Specialist I"
- Adam Gates has accepted a Supervisor position within the Warehouse and is no longer a Packer. All warehouse employees report to the two Supervisors and all office employees report to the Manager.

12. Amy Jones tried to send an e-mail to Adam Gates, but it wouldn't send.
    Which of the following offers the BEST explanation?
    A. Amy put Adam's first name first and then his last name.
    B. Adam doesn't check his e-mail, so he wouldn't know if he received the e-mail or not.
    C. Adam does not have his own e-mail.
    D. Office employees are not allowed to send e-mails to each other.

    12._____

13. How many Packers currently work for Apex Industries?
    A. 2   B. 3   C. 4   D. 5

    13._____

14. What position does Lisa Wong currently hold?
    A. Specialist I   B. Secretary
    C. Administrative Assistant   D. Loader

    14._____

15. If an employee wanted to contact the office manager, which of the following e-mails should the e-mail be sent to?
    A. officemanager@apexindustries.com
    B. brucelavine@apexindustries.com
    C. lavinebruce@apexindustries.com
    D. distribution@apexindustries.com

15.____

Questions 16-19.

DIRECTIONS: In answering Questions 16 through 19, compare the three names, numbers or addresses.

16. Smiley Yarnell   Smiley Yarnel   Smily Yarnell
    A. All three are exactly alike.
    B. The first and second are exactly alike.
    C. The second and third are exactly alike.
    D. All three are different.

16.____

17. 1583 Theater Drive   1583 Theater Drive   1583 Theatre Drive
    A. All three are exactly alike.
    B. The first and second are exactly alike.
    C. The second and third are exactly alike.
    D. All three are different.

17.____

18. 3341893212   3341893212   3341893212
    A. All three are exactly alike.
    B. The first and second are exactly alike.
    C. The second and third are exactly alike.
    D. All three are different.

18.____

19. Douglass Watkins   Douglas Watkins   Douglass Watkins
    A. All three are exactly alike.
    B. The first and third are exactly alike.
    C. The second and third are exactly alike.
    D. All three are different.

19.____

Questions 20-24.

DIRECTIONS: In answering Questions 20 through 24, you will be presented with a word. Choose the synonym that BEST represents the word in question.

20. Flexible
    A. delicate   B. inflammable   C. strong   D. pliable

20.____

21. Alternative
    A. choice   B. moderate   C. lazy   D. value

21.____

5 (#4)

22. Corroborate 22.____
    A. examine   B. explain   C. verify   D. explain

23. Respiration 23.____
    A. recovery   B. breathing   C. sweating   D. selfish

24. Negligent 24.____
    A. lazy   B. moderate   C. hopeless   D. lax

25. Plumber is to Wrench as Painter is to 25.____
    A. pipe   B. shop   C. hammer   D. brush

KEY (CORRECT ANSWERS)

1. D   11. A
2. A   12. C
3. D   13. A
4. C   14. A
5. B   15. C

6. C   16. D
7. C   17. B
8. B   18. A
9. C   19. B
10. C   20. D

21. A
22. C
23. B
24. D
25. D

NAME AND NUMBER COMPARISONS

COMMENTARY

This test seeks to measure your ability and disposition to do a job carefully and accurately, your attention to exactness and preciseness of detail, your alertness and versatility in discerning similarities and differences between things, and your power in systematically handling written language symbols.

It is actually a test of your ability to do academic and/or clerical work, using the basic elements of verbal (qualitative) and mathematical (quantitative) learning—words <u>and</u> numbers.

EXAMINATION SECTION

TEST 1

DIRECTIONS: Questions 1 through 6 consist of sets of names and addresses. In each question, the name and address in Column II should be an exact copy of the name and address in Column II. *PRINT IN THE SPACE AT THE RIGHT THE LETTER*
    A. if there is a mistake only in the name
    B. if there is a mistake only in the address
    C. if there is a mistake in both name and address
    D. If there is no mistake in either name or address

SAMPLE:
Michael Filbert	Michael Filbert
456 Reade Street	644 Reade Street
New York, N.Y. 10013	New York, N.Y. 10013

Since there is a mistake only in the address, the answer is B.

1.	Esta Wong 141 West 68 St. New York, N.Y. 10023	Esta Wang 141 West 68 St. New York, N.Y. 10023	1.____
2.	Dr. Alberto Grosso 3475 12th Avenue Brooklyn, N.Y. 11218	Dr. Alberto Grosso 3475 12th Avenue Brooklyn, N.Y. 11218	2.____
3.	Mrs. Ruth Bortlas 482 Theresa Ct. Far Rockaway, N.Y. 11691	Ms. Ruth Bortias 482 Theresa Ct. Far Rockaway, N.Y. 11169	3.____
4.	Mr. and Mrs. Howard Fox 2301 Sedgwick Ave. Bronx, N.Y. 10468	Mr. and Mrs. Howard Fox 231 Sedgwick Ave. Bronx, N.Y. 10468	4.____
5.	Miss Marjorie Black 223 East 23 Street New York, N.Y. 10010	Miss Margorie Black 223 East 23 Street New York, N.Y. 10010	5.____

2 (#1)

6. Michelle Herman   Michelle Hermann   6.____
   806 Valley Rd.   806 Valley Dr.
   Old Tappan, N.J. 07675   Old Tappan, N.J. 07675

KEY (CORRECT ANSWERS)

1. A
2. D
3. C
4. B
5. A
6. C

TEST 2

DIRECTIONS: Questions 1 through 6 consist of sets of names and addresses. In each question, the name and address in Column II should be an exact copy of the name and address in Column II. *PRINT IN THE SPACE AT THE RIGHT THE LETTER*
- A. if there is a mistake only in the name
- B. if there is a mistake only in the address
- C. if there is a mistake in both name and address
- D. If there is no mistake in either name or address

1.	Ms. Joan Kelly 313 Franklin Ave. Brooklyn, N.Y. 11202	Ms. Joan Kielly 318 Franklin Ave. Brooklyn, N.Y. 11202	1.____
2.	Mrs. Eileen Engel 47-24 86 Road Queens, N.Y. 11122	Mrs. Ellen Engel 47-24 86 Road Queens, N.Y. 11122	2.____
3.	Marcia Michaels 213 E. 81 St. New York, N.Y. 10012	Marcia Michaels 213 E. 81 St. New York, N.Y. 10012	3.____
4.	Rev. Edward J. Smyth 1401 Brandeis Street San Francisco, Calif. 96201	Rev. Edward J. Smyth 1401 Brandies Street San Francisco, Calif. 96201	4.____
5.	Alicia Rodriguez 24-68 81 St. Elmhurst, N.Y. 11122	Alicia Rodriquez 2468 81 St. Elmhurst, N.Y. 11122	5.____
6.	Ernest Eissemann 21 Columbia St. New York, N.Y. 10007	Ernest Eisermann 21 Columbia St. New York, N.Y. 10007	6.____

KEY (CORRECT ANSWERS)

1. C
2. A
3. D
4. B
5. C
6. A

TEST 3

DIRECTIONS: Questions 1 through 8 consist of names, locations, and telephone numbers. In each question, the name, location and number in Column II should be an exact copy of the name, location, and number in Column I. *PRINT IN THE SPACE AT THE RIGHT THE LETTER*
- A. if there is a mistake in one line only
- B. if there is a mistake in two lines only
- C. if there is a mistake in three lines only
- D. if there are no mistakes in any of the lines

1. Ruth Lang
   EAM Bldg., Room C101
   625-2000, ext. 765

   Ruth Lang
   EAM Bldg., Room C110
   625-2000, ext. 765
   1.____

2. Anne Marie Ionozzi
   Investigations, Room 827
   576-4000, ext. 832

   Anna Marie Ionozzi
   Investigation, Room 827
   566-4000, ext. 832
   2.____

3. Willard Jameson
   Fm C Bldg. Room 687
   454-3010

   Willard Jamieson
   Fm C Bldg. Room 687
   454-3010
   3.____

4. Joanne Zimmermann
   Bldg. SW, Room 314
   532-4601

   Joanne Zimmermann
   Bldg. SW, Room 314
   532-4601
   4.____

5. Carlyle Whetstone
   Payroll Division-A, Room 212A
   262-5000, ext. 471

   Caryle Whetstone
   Payroll Division-A, Room 212A
   262-5000, ext. 417
   5.____

6. Kenneth Chiang
   Legal Council, Room 9745
   (201) 416-9100, ext. 17

   Kenneth Chiang
   Legal Counsel, Room 9745
   (201) 416-9100, ext. 17
   6.____

7. Ethel Koenig
   Personnel Services Div, Rm 433
   635-7572

   Ethel Hoenig
   Personal Services Div, Rm 433
   635-7527
   7.____

8. Joyce Ehrhardt
   Office of Administrator, Rm W56
   387-8706

   Joyce Ehrhart
   Office of Administrator, Rm W56
   387-7806
   8.____

KEY (CORRECT ANSWERS)

1. A
2. C
3. A
4. D
5. B

6. A
7. C
8. B

TEST 4

DIRECTIONS: Each of Questions 1 through 10 gives the identification number and name of a person who has received treatment at a certain hospital. You are to choose the option (A, B, C, or D) which has EXACTLY the same number and name as those given in the question.

SAMPLE QUESTION:
123765 Frank Y. Jones
   A. 123675 Frank Y. Jones
   B. 123765 Frank T. Jones
   C. 123765 Frank Y. Jones
   D. 123765 Frank Y. Jones

The correct answer is D, because it is the only option showing the identification number and name exactly as they are in the sample question.

1. 754898 Diane Malloy
   A. 745898 Diane Malloy   B. 754898 Dion Malloy
   C. 754898 Diane Malloy   D. 754898 Diane Maloy

2. 661818 Ferdinand Figueroa
   A. 661818 Ferdinand Figeuroa   B. 661618 Ferdinand Figueroa
   C. 661818 Ferdnand Figueroa   D. 661818 Ferdinand Figueroa

3. 100101 Norman D. Braustein
   A. 100101 Norman D. Braustein   B. 101001 Norman D. Braustein
   C. 100101 Norman P. Braustien   D. 100101 Norman D. Bruastein

4. 838696 Robert Kittredge
   A. 838969 Robert Kittredge   B. 838696 Robert Kittredge
   C. 388696 Robert Kittredge   D. 838696 Robert Kittridge

5. 243716 Abraham Soletsky
   A. 243716 Abrahm Soletsky   B. 243716 Abraham Solestky
   C. 243176 Abraham Soletsky   D. 243716 Abraham Soletsky

6. 981121 Phillip M. Maas
   A. 981121 Phillip M. Mass   B. 981211 Phillip M. Maas
   C. 981121 Phillip M. Maas   D. 981121 Phillip N. Maas

7. 786556 George Macalusso
   A. 785656 George Macalusso   B. 786556 George Macalusso
   C. 786556 George Maculusso   D. 786556 George Macluasso

8. 639472 Eugene Weber
   A. 639472 Eugene Weber   B. 639472 Eugene Webre
   C. 693472 Eugene Weber   D. 639742 Eugene Weber

2 (#4)

9. 724936 John J. Lomonaco   9.____
   A. 724936 John J. Lomanoco   B. 724396 John L. Lomonaco
   C. 7224936 John J. Lomonaco   D. 724936 John J. Lamonaco

10. 899868 Michael Schnitzer   10.____
    A. 899868 Micheal Schnitzer   B. 898968 Michael Schnizter
    C. 899688 Michael Schnitzer   D. 899868 Michael Schnitzer

KEY (CORRECT ANSWERS)

1. C   6. C
2. D   7. B
3. A   8. A
4. B   9. C
5. D   10. D

NAME AND NUMBER CHECKING
EXAMINATION SECTION
TEST 1

DIRECTIONS: This test is designed to measure your speed/and accuracy. You are urged to work both quickly and accurately and to do correctly as many lists as you can in the time allowed. The test consists of lists or pairs of names and numbers. Count the number of IDENTICAL pairs in each list. Then, select the correct number, 1, 2, 3, 4, 5, and indicate your choice in the space at the right. Two sample questions are presented for your guidance, together with the correct solutions.

SAMPLE LIST A
Adelphi College — Adelphia College
Braxton Corp — Braxeton Corp.
Wassaic State School — Wassaic State School
Central Islip State Hospital — Central Isllip State Hospital
Greenwich House — Greenwich House

NOTE: There are only two correct pairs—Wassaic State School and Greenwich House. Therefore, the CORRECT answer is 2.

SAMPLE LIST B
78453694 — 78453684
784530 — 784530
533 — 534
67845 — 67845
2368745 — 2368755

NOTE: There are only two correct pairs—784530 and 67845. Therefore, the CORRECT answer is 2.

LIST 1   1.____
  98654327   - 98654327
  74932564   - 7492564
  61438652   - 61438652
  01297653   - 01287653
  1865439765   - 1865439765

LIST 2   2.____
  478362   - 478363
  278354792   - 278354772
  9327   - 9327
  297384625   - 27384625
  6428156   - 6428158

LIST 3
    Abbey House   - Abbey House
    Actor's Fund Home   - Actor's Fund Home
    Adrian Memorial   - Adrian Memorial
    A. Clayton Powell Home   - Clayton Powell House
    Abbot E. Kittredge Club   - Abbott E. Kitteredge Club

3.____

LIST 4
    3682   - 3692
    21937453829   - 31927453829
    723   - 733
    2763920   - 2763920
    47293   - 47293

4.____

LIST 5
    Adra House   - Adra House
    Adolescents' Court   - Adolescents' Court
    Cliff Villa   - Cliff Villa
    Clark Neighborhood House - Clark Neighborhood House
    Alma Mathews House   - Alma Mathews House

5.____

LIST 6
    28734291   - 28734271
    63810263849   - 63810263846
    26831027   - 26831027
    368291   - 368291
    7238102637   - 7238102637

6.____

LIST 7
    Albion State T.S.   - Albion State T.C.
    Clara de Hirsch Home   - Clara De Hirsch Home
    Alice Carrington Royce   - Alice Carington Royce
    Alice Chopin Nursery   - Alice Chapin Nursery
    Lighthouse Eye Clinic   - Lighthouse Eye Clinic

7.____

LIST 8
    327   - 329
    712438291026   - 712438291026
    2753829142   - 275382942
    826287   - 826289
    26435162839   - 26435162839

8.____

LIST 9
    Letchworth Village   - Letchworth Village
    A.A.A.E. Inc.   - A.A.A.E. Inc.
    Clear Pool Camp   - Clear Pool Camp
    A.M.M.L.A. Inc.   - A.M.M.L.A. Inc.
    J.G. Harbard   - J.G. Harbord

9.____

3 (#1)

LIST 10   10.____
    8254   - 8256
    2641526   - 2641526
    4126389012   - 4126389102
    725   - 725
    76253917287   - 76253917287

LIST 11   11.____
    Attica State Prison   - Attica State Prison
    Nellie Murrah   - Nellie Murrah
    Club Marshall   - Club Marshal
    Assissium Casea-Maria   - Assissium Casa-Maria
    The Homestead   - The Homestead

LIST 12   12.____
    2691   - 2691
    623819253627   - 623819253629
    28637   - 28937
    278392736   - 278392736
    52739   - 52739

LIST 13   13.____
    A.I.C.P. Boys Camp   - A.I.C.P. Boy's Camp
    Einar Chrystie   - Einar Christyie
    Astoria Center   - Astoria Center
    G. Frederick Brown   - G. Federick Browne
    Vacation Service   - Vacation Services

LIST 14   14.____
    728352689   - 728352688
    643728   - 643728
    37829176   - 37827196
    8425367   - 8425369
    65382018   - 65382018

LIST 15   15.____
    E.S. Streim   - E.S. Strim
    Charles E. Higgins   - Charles E. Higgins
    Baluvelt, N.Y.   - Blauwelt, N.Y.
    Roberta Magdalen   - Roberto Magdalen
    Ballard School   - Ballard School

LIST 16   16.____
    7382   - 7392
    281374538299   - 291374538299
    623   - 633
    6273730   - 6273730
    63392   - 63392

LIST 17
- Orrin Otis — - Orrin Otis
- Barat Settlement — - Barat Settlemen
- Emmanuel House — - Emmanuel House
- William T. McCreery — - William T. McCreery
- Seamen's Home — - Seaman's Home

17.____

LIST 18
- 72824391 — - 72834371
- 3729106237 — - 37291106237
- 82620163849 — - 82620163846
- 37638921 — - 37638921
- 82631027 — - 82631027

18.____

LIST 19
- Commonwealth Fund — - Commonwealth Fund
- Anne Johnsen — - Anne Johnson
- Bide-A-Wee Home — - Bide-a-Wee Home
- Riverdale-on-Hudson — - Riverdal-on-Hudson
- Bialystoker Home — - Bailystoker Home

19.____

LIST 20
- 9271 — - 9271
- 392918352627 — - 392018852629
- 72637 — - 72637
- 927392736 — - 927392736
- 92739 — - 92739

20.____

LIST 21
- Charles M. Stump — - Charles M. Stump
- Bourne Workshop — - Buorne Workshop
- B'nai Bi'rith — - B'nai Brith
- Poppenhuesen Institute — - Poppenheusen Institute
- Consular Service — - Consular Service

21.____

LIST 22
- 927352689 — - 927352688
- 647382 — - 648382
- 93729176 — - 93727196
- 649536718 — - 649536718
- 5835367 — - 5835369

22.____

LIST 23
- L.S. Bestend — - L.S. Bestent
- Hirsch Mfg. Co. — - Hircsh Mfg. Co.
- F.H. Storrs — - F.P. Storrs
- Camp Wassaic — - Camp Wassaic
- George Ballingham — - George Ballingham

23.____

5 (#1)

LIST 24
   372846392048   - 372846392048
   334   - 334
   7283524678   - 7283524678
   7283   - 7283
   7283629372   - 7283629372

24.____

LIST 25
   Dr. Stiles Company   - Dr. Stills Company
   Frances Hunsdon   - Frances Hunsdon
   Northrop Barrert   - Nothrup Barrent
   J.D. Brunjes   - J.D. Brunjes
   Theo. Claudel & Co.   - Theo. Claudel co.

25.____

KEY (CORRECT ANSWERS)

1.	3	11.	3
2.	1	12.	3
3.	2	13.	1
4.	2	14.	2
5.	5	15.	2
6.	3	16.	2
7.	1	17.	3
8.	2	18.	2
9.	4	19.	2
10.	3	20.	4

21. 2
22. 1
23. 2
24. 5
25. 2

TEST 2

DIRECTIONS: This test is designed to measure your speed/and accuracy. You are urged to work both quickly and accurately and to do correctly as many lists as you can in the time allowed. The test consists of lists or pairs of names and numbers. Count the number of IDENTICAL pairs in each list. Then, select the correct number, 1, 2, 3, 4, 5, and indicate your choice in the space at the right.

LIST 1   1.____
    82728   - 82738
    82736292637   - 82736292639
    728   - 738
    83926192527   - 83726192529
    82736272   - 82736272

LIST 2   2.____
    L. Pietri   - L. Pietri
    Mathewson, L.F.   - Mathewson, L.F.
    Funk & Wagnall   - Funk & Wagnalls
    Shimizu, Sojio   - Shimizu, Sojio
    Filing Equipment Bureau - Filing Equipment Buraeu

LIST 3   3.____
    63801829374   - 63801839474
    283577657   - 283577657
    65689   - 65689
    3457892026   - 3547893026
    2779   - 2778

LIST 4   4.____
    August Caille   - August Caille
    The Well-Fare Service   - The Wel-Fare Service
    K.L.M. Process co.   - R.L.M. Process Co.
    Merrill Littell   - Merrill Littell
    Dodd & Sons   - Dodd & Son

LIST 5   5.____
    998745732   - 998745733
    723   - 723
    463849102983   - 463849102983
    8570   - 8570
    279012   - 279012

LIST 6   6.____
    M.A. Wender   - M.A. Winder
    Minneapolis Supply Co. - Minneapolis Supply Co.
    Beverly Hills Corp   - Beverley Hills Corp.
    Trafalgar Square   - Trafalgar Square
    Phifer, D.T.   - Phiefer, D.T.

2 (#2)

LIST 7   7._____
    7834629   - 7834629
    3549806746   - 3549806746
    97802564   - 97892564
    689246   - 688246
    2578024683   - 2578024683

LIST 8   8._____
    Scadrons'   - Scadrons'
    Gensen & Bro.   - Genson & Bro.
    Firestone Co.   - Firestone Co.
    H.L. Eklund   - H.L. Eklund
    Oleomargarine Co.   - Oleomargarine Co.

LIST 9   9._____
    782039485618   - 782039485618
    53829172639   - 63829172639
    892   - 892
    82937482   - 829374820
    52937456   - 53937456

LIST 10   10._____
    First Nat'l Bank   - First Nat'l Bank
    Sedgwick Machine Works - Sedgewick Machine Works
    Hectographia Co.   - Hectographia Corp.
    Levet Bros.   - Levet Bros.
    Multistamp Co., Inc. - Multistamp Co., Inc.

LIST 11   11._____
    7293   - 7293
    6382910293   - 6382910292
    981928374012   - 981928374912
    58293   - 58393
    18203649271   - 283019283745

LIST 12   12._____
    Lowrey Lb'r Co.   - Lowrey Lb'r Co.
    Fidelity Service   - Fidelity Service
    Reumann, J.A.   - Reumann, J.A.
    Duophoto Ltd.   - Duophotos Ltd.
    John Jarratt   - John Jaratt

LIST 13   13._____
    6820384   - 6820384
    383019283745   - 383019283745
    63927102   - 63928102
    91029354829   - 91029354829
    58291728   - 58291728

LIST 14

    Standard Press Co.   - Standard Press Co.
    Reliant Mf'g. Co.   - Relant Mf'g Co.
    M.C. Lynn   - M.C. Lynn
    J. Fredericks Company   - G. Fredericks Company
    Wandermann, B.S.   - Wanderman, B.S.

14.____

LIST 15

    4283910293   - 4283010203
    992018273648   - 992018273848
    620   - 629
    752937273   - 752937373
    5392   - 5392

15.____

LIST 16

    Waldorf Hotel   - Waldorf Hotel
    Aaron Machinery Co.   - Aaron Machinery Co.
    Caroline Ann Locke   - Caroline Ane Locke
    McCabe Mfg. Co.   - McCabe Mfg. Co.
    R.L. Landres   - R.L. Landers

16.____

LIST 17

    68391028364   - 68391028394
    68293   - 68293
    739201   - 739201
    72839201   - 72839211
    739917   - 739719

17.____

LIST 18

    Balsam M.M.   - Balsamm, M.M.
    Steinway & Co.   - Stienway & M. Co.
    Eugene Elliott   - Eugene A. Elliott
    Leonard Loan Co.   - Leonard Loan Co.
    Frederick Morgan   - Frederick Morgen

18.____

LIST 19

    8929   - 9820
    392836472829   - 392836572829
    462   - 4622039271
    827   - 2039276837
    53829   - 54829

19.____

LIST 20

    Danielson's Hofbrau   - Danielson's Hafbrau
    Edward A. Truarme   - Edward A. Truame
    Insulite Co.   - Insulite Co.
    Reisler Shoe Corp.   - Rielser Shoe Corp.
    L.L. Thompson   - L.L. Thompson

20.____

4 (#2)

LIST 21   21._____
    92839102837   - 92839102837
    58891028   - 58891028
    7291728   - 7291928
    272839102839   - 272839102839
    428192   - 428102

LIST 22   22._____
    K.L. Veiller   - K.L. Veiller
    Webster, Roy   - Webster, Ray
    Drasner Spring Co.   - Drasner Spring Co.
    Edward J. Cravenport   - Edward J. Cravanport
    Harold Field   - Harold A. Field

LIST 23   23._____
    2293   - 2293
    4283910293   - 5382910292
    871928374012   - 871928374912
    68293   - 68393
    8120364927   - 81293649271

LIST 24   24._____
    Tappe, Inc   - Tappe, Inc.
    A.M. Wentingworth   - A.M. Wentinworth
    Scott A. Elliott   - Scott A. Elliott
    Echeverria Corp.   - Echeverria Corp.
    Bradford Victor Company - Bradford Victer Company

LIST 25   25._____
    4820384   - 4820384
    393019283745   - 283919283745
    63917102   - 63927102
    91029354829   - 91029354829
    48291728   - 48291728

KEY (CORRECT ANSWERS)

1.	1	11.	1
2.	3	12.	3
3.	2	13.	4
4.	2	14.	2
5.	4	15.	1
6.	2	16.	3
7.	3	17.	2
8.	4	18.	1
9.	2	19.	1
10.	3	20.	2

21. 3
22. 2
23. 1
24. 2
25. 4

www.ingramcontent.com/pod-product-compliance
Lightning Source LLC
Chambersburg PA
CBHW082207300426
44117CB00016B/2706